TO UNDERSTAND
THE
WORLD,

TO SAVE
THE
WORLD

Christian Mission and Modern Culture

EDITED BY
ALAN NEELY, H. WAYNE PIPKIN,
AND WILBERT R. SHENK

In the Series:

TO UNDERSTAND

THE

WORLD,

TO SAVE

THE

WORLD

THE INTERFACE BETWEEN MISSIOLOGY AND THE SOCIAL SCIENCES

CHARLES R. TABER

TRINITY PRESS
INTERNATIONAL
HARRISBURG, PENNSYLVANIA

Trinity Press International, P.O. Box 1321, Harrisburg, PA 17105

Trinity Press International is a division of the Morehouse Group.

Scripture quotations are from the New Revised Standard Version Bible, copyright 1989, Division of Christian Education of the National Council of the Churches of Christ in the United States of America, and are used by permission.

Library of Congress Cataloging-in-Publication Data
Taber, Charles R.
    To understand the world, to save the world : the interface between missiology and the social sciences / Charles R. Taber.
        p. cm. — (Christian mission and modern culture)
    Includes bibliographical references.
    ISBN 1-56338-316-0 (pbk.)
    1. Missions—Theory.   2. Christianity and the social sciences.   I. Title.   II. Series.
BV2063 .T27 2000
266'.001—dc21   00–025307

Printed in the United States of America

00 01 02 03 04 05 6 5 4 3 2 1

*For my teachers at the Hartford Seminary Foundation,
especially H. A. Gleason, Jr.,
and
my colleagues in the United Bible Societies,
especially Eugene A. Nida*

Contents

Preface to the Series

Both Christian mission and modern culture, widely regarded as antagonists, are in crisis. The emergence of the modern mission movement in the early nineteenth century cannot be understood apart from the rise of technocratic society. Now, at the beginning of the twenty-first century, both modern culture and Christian mission face an uncertain future.

One of the developments integral to modernity was the way the role of religion in culture was redefined. Whereas religion had played an authoritative role in the culture of Christendom, modern culture was highly critical of religion and increasingly secular in its assumptions. A sustained effort was made to banish religion to the backwaters of modern culture.

The decade of the 1980s witnessed further momentous developments on the geopolitical front with the collapse of communism. In the aftermath of the breakup of the system of power blocs that dominated international relations for a generation, it is clear that religion has survived even if its institutionalization has undergone deep change and its future forms are unclear. Secularism continues to oppose religion, while technology has emerged as a major source of power and authority in modern culture. Both confront Christian faith with fundamental questions.

The purpose of this series is to probe these developments from a variety of angles with a view to helping the

church understand its missional responsibility to a culture
in crisis. One important resource is the church's experience of two centuries of cross-cultural mission that has
reshaped the church into a global Christian *ecumene.* The
focus of our inquiry will be the church in modern culture. The series (1) examines modern/postmodern culture from a missional point of view; (2) develops the
theological agenda that the church in modern culture must
address in order to recover its own integrity; and (3) tests
fresh conceptualizations of the nature and mission of the
church as it engages modern culture. In other words, these
volumes are intended to be a forum where conventional
assumptions can be challenged and alternative formula-
tions explored.

This series is a project authorized by the Institute of
Mennonite Studies, research agency of the Associated
Mennonite Biblical Seminary, and supported by a generous
grant from the Pew Charitable Trusts.

Editorial Committee

ALAN NEELY
H. WAYNE PIPKIN
WILBERT R. SHENK

Acknowledgments

No book is the unassisted work of a single person, least of all this one. In addition to the huge debts acknowledged in the References Cited section, and no doubt the inadvertently unacknowledged use of ideas whose origins I have forgotten, I am deeply beholden to several persons who have given me invaluable help—some by suggesting readings and ideas, and all by reading the entire manuscript critically. I want, therefore, to thank the following persons: Dwight P. Baker, Donna K. Dial, Susan G. Higgins, Charles S. Taber, and Wilbert R. Shenk. They have individually and collectively saved me from numerous errors; such errors and weaknesses as remain doubtless occur at points where I declined to follow their advice.

Missiological Prelude

The purpose of this series is to develop a missiology of Western culture; that is, an understanding of the Western world that will in turn inform a strategy for addressing the gospel of the kingdom of God to that world relevantly, intelligibly, and persuasively. The understanding must be seen to be crucial to the efficacy of the strategy, in the West, just as it has been, at least in intention, in earlier missionary efforts to address the non-Western world.

But the West and its social structures and cultures constitute a highly complex and heterogeneous reality. Because we missiologists are for the most part Westerners, members of that reality, we not only benefit from insiders' knowledge and insight, but are also shaped, often warped, always limited, by the specific, taken-for-granted worldviews into which we are born. In such a situation, we need all the help, all the tools we can find to correct and deepen our understanding. Some missiologists will, quite appropriately, look to history, philosophy, and literature for such help. This volume looks to the social sciences—sociology, anthropology, psychology, economics, political science—for whatever assistance they can afford.

The thesis of this volume is threefold. First, missiology up to the present has established links almost exclusively with cultural/social anthropology, largely to the neglect of the other social sciences. This is because both missiology and anthropology have focused chiefly on the exotic (as viewed from a Western stance) and even the so-called primitive societies of the world. Second, although this interaction has had a number of very valuable and valid dimensions, it has been on the whole superficial and uncritical. Third, in designing a missiology for the Western world, the social sciences cannot only provide very helpful tools of insight and understanding, as has been the case in the missiology of the exotic, non-Western world; they can also give expression in themselves, in concentrated and intellectualized form, to a number of aspects of the modern and postmodern Western worldviews. They are therefore symptomatic of the nature of Western culture. In other words, they both arise from the common spirit of the age, sharpening certain of its traits; and they in turn are refracted, often in grossly reduced and distorted ways, in the popular worldview. They can be—often indirectly— immensely influential in shaping the beliefs, values, attitudes, and actions of persons and groups. Anyone wanting to understand the modern and postmodern worlds, therefore, cannot neglect the social sciences, which have in many ways, together with their senior cousins, the natural sciences, replaced philosophy as the arena in which the world's ideas are shaped. A missiology that intends to address the inhabitants of the contemporary Western world, that hopes to make the gospel in all its integrity and power intelligible and persuasive in that world, must arm itself with a penetrating and critical understanding of the social sciences, using them both as tools of interpretation and as symptoms of what is to be understood.

In developing these theses, I will deal first with the long historical background against which both missiology and the social sciences arose as formal disciplines in the nineteenth and twentieth centuries. Next, I will consider the actual emergence of the disciplines themselves and their interaction in the past two centuries. Finally, I will discuss a number of issues raised within the social sciences that constitute in my judgment the heart of the missiological agenda of the church in addressing the Western world, and will offer some cautious suggestions as to how missiology ought to tackle them.

It may seem at times that I am denouncing the social sciences *in toto* as mistaken, if not actually evil. What I am trying to do is to present a balanced picture, showing positively how these disciplines help us better understand our world, but negatively how they sometimes are subject to, or produce, ideological or other constraints that come into conflict with a biblically informed understanding. It will also be noted that none of the social sciences enjoys perfect unanimity among its practitioners, so that for many of my caveats there are also balancing points of commendation.

It should be made clear that this is not an exhaustive history or analysis of the subject matter; it is an interpretation. Because this is the case, I will focus on the specific major issues that are relevant to my purpose and will draw in broad strokes the figures and ideas involved. For the rest, I will select a small but representative sample of the available material. Hundreds of names and titles that necessarily appeared in major works such as Harris (1968) and Milbank (1990) will pass unmentioned here.

I begin by observing, then, that long before there was "missiology" or "missiologists," there were missions and missionaries; and long before there were "social sciences" and "social scientists," there were perceptive and profound examinations made of the human condition. We must, therefore, do a bit of history before tackling the subject matter proper of this volume.

1

Historical Background

Introduction

Karl Marx wrote that "philosophers have only interpreted the world in various ways; the point is to change it" (*Theses on Feuerbach*, 1888). I have chosen to entitle this volume *To Understand the World, to Save the World* in order to suggest a somewhat analogous relationship between missiology and the social sciences—sociology, anthropology, psychology, economics, political science—sometimes also called the behavioral or human sciences. In the current scene at least, it does seem to be the self-appointed task of the social sciences to try to understand the world while quite often eschewing any claim to utility in changing the world, and the God-appointed task of missions to labor for the salvific transformation of the world.

But the social sciences have not always been "objective" and uncommitted. In fact, as we will see, when they emerged from the matrix of the Enlightenment, they had quite utopian and even messianic ambitions. John Locke, Adam Smith, and a number of the philosophers of the eighteenth century in France laid the foundations for the social sciences. Those who formulated the purposes and ideals of both the American and the French revolutions explicitly relied on the ideas of these proto-social scientists. In the nineteenth century, the founders of the social sciences themselves—such as Saint-Simon and Comte in France; Thomas Malthus, David Ricardo, and J. S. Mill in England; and especially Karl Marx—aimed explicitly to develop the ideal society by the use of their knowledge and the power it would confer on them.

But sometime in the transition from the nineteenth century to the twentieth, and especially after World War I, the engaged, ameliorative stance of the infant social sciences rather rapidly diminished, to be largely replaced by the notion of "value-free" and "objective" science. Both David H. Hopper (1991) and Stanford M. Lyman (1978) have, as we will see, documented this enormous shift. Why the shift in self-understanding from the actively utopian to the detached, objective attitude? Two major causes seem to have been at work. On the one hand, as Lyman points out, "sociological optimism was a major casualty of World War I" (1978:2). The arrogant self-confidence of the nineteenth century gave way, especially in Europe, to grave self-doubts about the ability of humans to engineer any viable utopia. This new pessimism was perhaps best articulated by the German Oswald Spengler in his *The Decline of the West* (English trans. 1934). Hopper (1991) makes the somewhat different but not incompatible point that although the idea that progress should come through the political process declined drastically in the early part of this century, optimism about technological progress continued apace and even usurped the role of the political; in other words, people began to look to technology—both the technology of controlling things and the technology of controlling people—as basis for confidence in a better future.

On the other hand, it was also the case that the ambition to be scientific in the same sense as physics motivated many social scientists in their passage from the "moral philosophy" posture that prevailed in the eighteenth century to the "social science" posture in the latter part of the nineteenth century. These scholars determined at all costs to be objective, that is, detached and uninvolved, in exactly the same manner as the physical scientists. As part of the same strategy, they also moved away from a focus on purpose and ends (both anathema in the Enlightenment epistemology) to a cause-and-effect perspective, which led to a more rigorous preoccupation with means and mechanisms. These moves led by a very short step to determinism. The result is that when social scientists referred to social ends, even obliquely, they tended to do so either naively, or apologetically, or both. But recently there have been some significant shifts in the direction of a more nuanced and sophisticated stance. In particular, not a few social scientists today make an important place in their cause-and-effect pattern for human intentionality as itself a cause, thus escaping some forms of determinism. But teleology at the macro-level, such as appeal to the purposes of God as active in history, remains anathema. We will discuss the philosophical/theological issues involved in Chapter 5, but we can at least introduce some of them here.

What the social sciences study is what the New Testament calls "the world." The New Testament uses four different words to designate "the world," each of which has significance for the social sciences: (1) *ge*, "the physical earth," the object of study of geology and geography; (2) *oikoumene*, "the inhabited earth"; (3) *kosmos*, "order, structure, system" (a space image); and (4) *aion*, "age, era" (a time image). *Kosmos* synchronically evokes institutions; *aion* diachronically evokes the epochs of history. Science presents the world it studies as *sui generis*, a closed, self-contained system. Though the first origins of these things were the focus of considerable interest in the infant social sciences in the nineteenth century, more recently their attention has been directed either to how the social sciences function or to how they developed through time, *after* their origins.

The New Testament says of these things that (a) they were created good by God to make human life on earth secure and successful; (b) they were spoiled by the Fall; (c) they are at present ruled by a usurper, Satan (John 12:31); and (d) they are the object of God's liberating and restoring purpose (e.g., Acts 3:21; see Wink 1992). Wink suggests—correctly, I think—that each worldly reality exists at two levels: the empirically available level of structures and institutions, and the more hidden level of worldviews and ideologies (i.e., spirit), which serves to legitimate the overt systems and to explain how they work.

The social sciences also study, of course, what the New Testament calls "humanity," "humankind," and "human beings" (*anthropos*). As we will see, they often present human beings as (a) evolved from earlier organisms, notably earlier hominids, and therefore integrally a part of the animal kingdom, with no really significant gap between the human and other animal species; and, until recently, as (b) largely or totally determined by genes, environment, or both, leaving little room for real freedom. This is ironic, because it has from their beginning been part of the avowed agenda of the social sciences to free humans from all kinds of servitude—including servitude to God—and even all kinds of constraints and restraints on their impulses. The social sciences, as true children of the Enlightenment, also present humans as (c) monadic individuals, who are often fragmented between disparate and often incompatible social roles (see Douglas and Ney 1998).

The New Testament, on the other hand, presents humans as created in the image of God—rational, relational, moral, and free. But it explains much of the presence of evil in terms of human rebellion against God's rule in search of an illusory freedom and even an illusory godhead, which ironically led only to a lapse into slavery—slavery to the ruler of the world, slavery to personal passions and appetites.

What, then, is the relationship between missiology, the "science" of (Christian) missions, and the social sciences? What has it been historically, what is it today, and what can or should it be in the near future, especially in relation to developing a missiology of Western culture?

During the nineteenth century, relations between missionaries and social scientists—insofar as there were any—were exploratory and tentative, as each sought, if only occasionally, to understand the other's intentions. But it must be said that on the whole the scientists were often much more aware than the missionaries of the deep philosophical incompatibilities between them. Missionaries, after all, were explicitly or implicitly committed to the gospel of the kingdom of God, which looked to divine intervention to bring an ultimate happy resolution to the world's problems caused by human sin. Social scientists, on the other hand, in their more utopian moments looked to utopias built by human endeavor without the intervention of an otiose or nonexistent God; and in their more scientific moments, they either looked (optimistically) to immanent, inevitable progress within a closed universe or just plodded on (pessimistically) to try to understand the human condition without any expectation of amelioration. The closest that theology ever came to science in the optimistic nineteenth century was in postmillennial eschatological theology, which saw the Second Coming of Christ at the *end* of the millennium as God's ultimate expression of approval of the successful human effort to bring in the kingdom of God.

In the 1990s, on the other hand, the difference in motivation, intention, and style of action between missionaries and social scientists has contributed greatly to the ambivalent, dialectic, and often hostile relationship between missiology and the social sciences. From the point of view of anthropologists in particular, missionaries have been viewed as meddlers who contaminated the field of study and thus both spoiled "the natives" and undermined the validity of the anthropologists' findings. It is curious that the anthropologists rarely saw *themselves* as invasive! Anthropologists, increasingly committed to cultural relativism, have also roundly condemned the arrogance and ethnocentrism of missionaries who presumed that they were right and indigenous peoples were wrong about ultimate issues.

Missions

The responsibility and privilege of sharing the gospel of the kingdom of God with the peoples of the earth was understood not very long after Pentecost to be an inherent and essential dimension of the church's nature. This mission has now been pursued with varying degrees of assiduity and sloth, wisdom and folly, and success and failure for about two millennia. But critical reflection on the task of mission, which constitutes the essence of missiology, has been episodic at best. Various Christian persons and groups have, however, from time to time given careful thought to how the church should relate missionally and missiologically to the world.

As a matter of fact, the apostolic church and the second-century apologists on the whole thought much harder about how they should relate to the societies and cultures in which they themselves lived than about how they should address foreign societies and cultures. Their *oikoumene*, the realm in which they struggled for survival and expression, was the Roman Empire, and regions outside that empire did not on the whole engage their attention. In other words, the most intense and sustained missiological reflection in the first two or three centuries of the church's life was concerned with what today would be called "home" missions. The church, in both East and West, continued as a matter of course to *do* mission outside the *oikoumene*. The Eastern church, for example, faced and to some extent addressed the vast ranges and teeming millions of Asia. The Nestorian mission in China (seventh to ninth centuries) is an outstanding case in point. The Western church also continued to do mission on the frontiers, but this was marginal to the church inside the empire. Nevertheless, one remembers the correspondence of Gregory the Great with the missionary team of Augustine of Canterbury, advising what we would today call "contextualization" in the mission to Great Britain in the seventh century. Neill quotes Gregory's letter as reported by the Venerable Bede in *Ecclesiastical History of the English Nation:*

> The heathen temples of these peoples need not be destroyed, only the idols which are to be found in them. . . . If the temples are well built, it is a good idea to detach them from the service of the devil, and to adapt them for the worship of the true God. . . . And since the people are accustomed, when they assemble for sacrifice, to kill many oxen in sacrifice to the devils, it seems reasonable to appoint a festival for the people by way of exchange (Neill 1964:68).

Gregory goes on to prescribe a number of additional concrete instances of what modern missiology, informed by cultural anthropology, would come to call functional substitutions. It is evident from the letter, however, that Gregory assumed a degree of coercive power that Augustine may not in fact have possessed, and that later missionaries fortunately do not usually have.

The reason for what became a growing gulf between theology and mission was that "Christendom" came into being in the fourth century A.D., when emperors became Christian and the Empire itself was therefore deemed to have become Christian. Mission and such slight missiological reflection

as was done were therefore redirected to focus exclusively
on the encounter of the church with alien societies and
cultures, and ceased to be concerned with the relations
between the church and its home environment, which, it
was assumed, was already Christian and therefore not a
field for mission. This mentality dominated the minds of
Christian thinkers up to our own day; Warneck (1901), for
instance, insisted on a clear distinction between mission,
which took place in the faraway "non-Christian" world,
and evangelism, which took place in "Christian" countries
and consisted largely in reclaiming lapsed Christians. (In
our day, this view has been espoused by Ralph D. Winter
and some others.) I should add that the terminology of
"mission" was not in use in any quarter to refer to efforts
to proclaim the gospel and to extend the church beyond its
current boundaries until the sixteenth century, when it
was so used by the Jesuits (Bosch 1991:228); but the effort
to extend the gospel was nevertheless being made. Nor am
I saying that theologians and prelates lost interest in relations between the church and its "home" context! On the
contrary, I am suggesting that the process that began very
early, by which theology and canon law came to deal
largely with the concerns of the home base while mission
and missiology came to address exclusively the distant and
the different, has continued to this day, as has been shown
by David J. Bosch (1991:489–92).

The Social Sciences

Just as missions and missionaries preceded by centuries
the emergence of missiology, so did acute observation and
perceptive description of alien societies and cultures, as
found in the works of Herodotus and Tacitus and other
ancient Greeks and Romans, precede the "social sciences"
and "social scientists." There seems not to have been as
much critical study of the classical societies and cultures
themselves, though several philosophers, notably Plato in

the *Republic* and Aristotle in various writings, concerned themselves with what the ideal society might be like. No doubt, arrogant ethnocentrism accounted in part for the general lack of critical self-evaluation; perhaps also the cautionary experience of Socrates gave pause to would-be critics of the domestic establishment. In the Roman world of the first century B.C. and the first century A.D., the period that saw the transition from republic to empire, confrontation and conflict over sheer de facto power seem to have drowned out serious critical reflection about Roman institutions, at least in the public arena.

Obviously, ever since human beings have existed, they have been curious about themselves and others and have made more or less profound and true observations about what they have seen when they have looked at themselves and others. It is part of the human condition to reflect self-consciously and to want to know and to understand. But it is significant that such study has become scientific in a specific sense only in the last two centuries. The modern period—that is, the period of history in Europe and its offshoots since the Renaissance—has been simultaneously (a) the period in which human beings have increasingly declared their autonomy from any external authority, including that of God; (b) the period in which the nation state has emerged and demanded autonomy from the church, especially after the disastrous "wars of religion" in the sixteenth and seventeenth centuries; (c) the period in which economic institutions developed toward modern capitalism; and (d) the period in which the knowledge of the empirically available world has mushroomed into formal disciplines called "sciences." The growing success of human beings in the scientific enterprise and its technological applications led to a growing self-confidence, which easily turned into arrogance, a sense that they could do almost anything without outside help, and especially without the help of God. Growing success also fed growing optimism, so that a future fully under human control seemed to promise inevitable and endless progress—the secular *eschaton* of the Enlightenment.

Something should be said at this point about the main lines of Enlightenment thought. I am guided in this discussion by the very thorough treatment of this theme by Bosch (1991:262–67), who saw seven traits as characterizing this era: (1) an emphasis on "reason" as a universal feature of humankind and as the foundation of all valid thought; (2) an emphasis on a "subject-object scheme," which permitted an objective, detached relation between the observing subject and the observed object, and also focused study upon the operation of analysis, which pays attention to parts rather than to wholes; (3) the "elimination of purpose" and its replacement by "cause-and-effect" as the correct manner of understanding reality, which replaced an open, future-driven point of view with a closed, past-driven point of view; (4) a touching faith in "progress" as inevitable, which replaced the Christian understanding of future possibilities with a purely secular understanding; (5) the notion that scientific knowledge was "factual, value-free, and neutral," that it "has a life of [its] own, independent of the observer," and that it stands in contrast with "values," which are unprovable matters of personal choice or preference; (6) the notion that "all problems were in principle solvable," which in effect called for a heavy emphasis on method and technique in approaching all questions; and finally (7) the view of persons as "emancipated, autonomous individuals," which greatly weakened all connections between persons, even the closest and most enduring. All of these traits of Enlightenment thought had their impact on the emerging understandings of the world, including the world of social connections and processes that came to be the subject matter, first of the "moral philosophy" approach to the human scene, then of the social sciences as they emerged in the nineteenth century.

Another way of describing the modern agenda is as follows, focusing on the concept of *universality* (see also Lasch 1991:124–26):

The fundamental unity of the human race was postulated over against the localisms and particularisms of the past (and also of Romanticism); this notion gave birth to subsidiary concepts, such as the "universal grammar" of the Port Royal grammarians in seventeenth-century France, the "universal rights of man" [*sic*] in the eighteenth century, the "psychic unity of mankind" [*sic*] . . . in the nineteenth century, and the "universal laws of economics" today. Ironically, even the rhetoric of universal human rights, to say nothing of the other notions mentioned, tended to exert in practice a ruthlessly homogenizing effect on societies and cultures as it was disseminated around the world in the colonial era. Today, it hardly needs mentioning that the homogenizing impact of the West on the rest of the world is driven chiefly by the forces of the global market, with its messianic illusions and false salvific claims. In many quarters in the West, the collapse of Marxism in eastern Europe has had as its chief effect to foster the disastrously unfortunate notion of the inevitability and infallibility of free market forces to solve all problems. We are currently seeing the fallout of this in Russia.

The moderns at their idealistic best desperately wanted to overcome the destructive effects of the divisions and particularisms of humankind and create one world of peace and order. After all, the terrible wars of religion were very vivid in their memories. But precisely because of those wars of religion, they saw faith in God as a divisive rather than unifying factor. So they aspired to reap the

fruits of faith in God on their own without God. But
the human predicament, as Genesis 3–4 points out,
begins precisely at the point where God's rule is
rejected in the name of human freedom. The human
declaration of independence from God leads automatically to either anarchy (Hobbes' "war, as of
every man, against every man"; cf. Cain and Abel,
Gen 4), or to the rule of the stronger over the weaker
(cf. Adam and Eve, Gen 3). The problem of any
human dream of order, local or universal, apart from
the rule of God, is this: if God is not acknowledged to
be in charge, then someone else is. Whether one is
talking about a monarch or a corporate CEO; about
an oligarchy, a patriarchy, a gerontocracy, a bureau-
cracy, or even the tyranny of "the market," the
dilemma is the same. . . . And if one looks at attempts
to ground power and authority in "the people"
(Locke, Rousseau, Jefferson, et al.), the result is also
deeply disappointing: whether in the Marxist version
of lockstep collectivism or in the "liberal" version of
an ad hoc assortment of free individuals, "the people" all too easily lend themselves to the tyranny of
the majority, or to manipulation by demagogues
(Taber: 2001).

We will explore in Chapter 5 the ways in which these perspectives offer both obstacles and opportunities for the
gospel.

With respect to the physical universe—the solar system
and its parts, galaxies and nebulae, on down to the world of
the molecule, the atom, and subatomic particles, and
everything in between, including living organisms—the
respective sciences have created a vast array of sophisticated theories and models, and from these theories they
have derived and tested hypotheses that have given us an
unprecedented knowledge of what things are made of and

of how they work. Even here, of course, as philosophers of science such as Polanyi (1958) and Kuhn (1970) have shown, the process has not been one of uninterrupted cumulative progress; there have been periodic major shifts of perspective, shifts in what Kuhn calls "paradigms," as from the Ptolemaic paradigm to the Copernican, then the Newtonian, then the Einsteinian. These shifts have involved the rejection of quite fundamental ideas that had been taken for granted before and the adoption by faith of new ideas, often in anticipation of their later empirical confirmation. But for the most part, taking a more or less empirical stance—that is, assuming that our physical senses and their instrumental extensions give us a reliable picture of the universe—has worked quite well.

The picture changes, however, as soon as one begins to wonder about those aspects and activities of human beings individually and collectively that mobilize realities that escape empirical observation: reason (what the ancient Greeks called *nous*), feelings and emotions, attitudes, choices, memory, imagination, consciousness and attention, communication and miscommunication, and their outcomes in agreement or disagreement. One can observe brains and their chemical and electrical activities; one can, in a very different sense, observe the external effects of the activities of mind. But one cannot in any serious sense specify the connections between brain and mind, whether at the level of an individual human being or in the interactions between human beings. Such terms as "person" (in a social sense) and "self" (in an individual sense), despite thousands of hours of study and experimentation and thousands of volumes published, remain mysterious. Empirical observation, experiment, and analysis seem to come up against very real barriers in addressing these realities.

One crucial difference between the physical sciences and the social sciences is that the latter are *reflexive*: that is, social scientists, studying the human scene, are themselves human beings inextricably enmeshed in their fields of study. Even across the barriers of very different cultures, anthropologists find themselves reacting as human beings in their relationships with the persons they are studying; in other words, their subjectivity gets into the picture willy-nilly. Most social scientists try to mask their subjective reactions, but this does not eliminate them. This fact makes objectivity quite a bit more problematical in the social sciences than in the physical sciences, as we will see later.

The Enlightenment, coming hard on the heels of the turmoil of the Reformation and counter-Reformation in the sixteenth and seventeenth centuries, as well as the explosion of knowledge derived from the exploration and colonization of faraway places, began to devote serious reflection to the nature of society and its institutions, which began for the first time to be seen as contingent rather than absolute, historically created rather than eternal, and humanly designed and managed rather than divinely given. Coinciding, for instance, with the first gradual steps in the self-conscious emergence of the nation state, we have the works of Machiavelli (*The Prince*, 1513) and Hobbes (*Leviathan*, 1651). Later, during the Enlightenment, there were the works of Locke (e.g., *Two Treatises of Government*, 1689), Montesquieu (*L'Esprit des lois*, 1748), and Rousseau (*Du Contrat social*, 1762). With respect to economics, as Tawney has shown (1926), various philosophers and theologians, including Luther and Calvin, had their say about proto-capitalism; but the decisive work describing and advocating pre-industrial capitalism was Adam Smith's *The Wealth of Nations* (1776). All of these people (except Luther and Calvin, who were of course doing theology) were, however, quite consciously doing philosophy—specifically "moral philosophy." They were, in other words, engaging in exploring in a widening panorama what we would today call social ethics.

Yet the basic ideas they advanced were the seedbed from which what came to be called the social sciences emerged later. Most of these thinkers, especially as the Enlightenment came into its full development, had a decidedly "missionary" and utopian complexion in that they aspired to design the ideal society by the application of the knowledge that they were accumulating and the theories that they were creating. It might be said, in fact, that they quite consciously offered the Western world an alternative, humanly-created *eschaton* in place of the kingdom of God, which is the essence of the Christian Good News. These thinkers were intoxicated with the notion that humans could understand their own situation well enough to be able to control their future. Both the American and French Revolutions were launched and powered by just such ideas.

The result was that when the social sciences, consciously so-called, began to emerge from the mid-nineteenth century on, they were established on very specific conceptual foundations. Included among these was a marked commitment to "Progress," both in evolutionary versions, which were conceived of as inevitable, and in utopian versions, which needed to be engineered by human beings. In fact, not a few of the nineteenth-century thinkers, Marx above all, tried to hold both of these views at once, apparently without sensing the contradiction. As Lyman has pointed out, for example: "Sociology was associated with the social construction not only of present-day realities but also of utopias" (1978:1).

2

Modern Missions and Missiology

History

Simultaneous with the passage in social studies from "moral philosophy" to "social science," the Protestant part of the modern missionary movement, delayed as it was for about two centuries after the Roman Catholic expansion, was itself also largely built upon Enlightenment foundations, albeit somewhat modified through the Christian understandings of its practitioners and supporters.

But missionary activity was of course much older than that. The tradition in the "Christian" West of interest in the exotic was continued in the first fourteen centuries A.D. by many travelers from the West, both missionaries and others. The missiologist Ramon Lull in the twelfth century explicitly drew upon what was known of Islam and the Islamic world, and demanded that that knowledge be intentionally expanded in order to design a missionary approach by which the gospel might be appropriately addressed to Muslims (Neill 1964:134–36).

Both missions and the knowledge of faraway cultures took an enormous leap in the fifteenth and sixteenth centuries, with Iberian imperial expansion and its burgeoning missionary dimension. Franciscans and Dominicans were early on the scene, and the Society of Jesus, founded by Ignatius de Loyola, became the first agency to use the terms *mission* and *missionary* or *missioner* in the sense we are familiar with today. Before the sixteenth century was over, this order had sent out an army of outstanding missionaries, chiefly to Asia, but also to Latin America. In India, then in Japan, Saint Francis Xavier was the extraordinary pioneer. Roberto de Nobili in India adapted his lifestyle to the demands of Brahmin taboos and presented Jesus as "the Guru"—an enormously creative effort in inculturation (Clooney 1990). In China, Matteo Ricci made his way in the imperial court and advocated a high degree of contextual adaptation, which won a hearing from the Chinese; but, after a long-drawn-out battle between Jesuits and Franciscans called the Rites Controversy, his initiatives were eventually forbidden by the Vatican (Neill 1964:163–65). In Indochina, it was Valignano, Rhodes, and their colleagues who laid the foundation for a durable Christian presence (Neill 1964:157–58, 195–97). In Latin America, missionaries provided the most thorough and profound descriptions of the numerous cultures they encountered in the New World—Aztecs, Incas, Hurons, and so forth. Lafitau's *Moeurs des sauvages amériquains comparées aux moeurs des premiers temps* (1724) can properly be credited with an early statement of the notion of primitivity (cf., the title of the work), as well as a first statement of cultural relativity. These descriptions, despite showing occasional evidences of blatant ethnocentrism and even dislike of the peoples they addressed, were usually characterized by surprising accuracy, profundity, and insight. But the eighteenth century saw a drastic decline in Roman Catholic missionary effort and was marked by the suppression of the Society of Jesus, which was not revived until the next century.

In the meantime, the Vatican had established the Congregation for the Propagation of the Faith (in Latin,

Propaganda Fide, 1622), which not only coordinated Roman Catholic missionary efforts around the world under the direct authority of the Pope, but also from time to time gave directives regarding the methods of mission work that we would today call contextualization or inculturation; it also stressed the necessity of respecting indigenous cultures and of forgoing any form of compulsion or coercion in mission.

After sporadic efforts in the seventeenth and eighteenth centuries by a few German Pietists, Moravians, and Anglicans, Protestant missions surged in the nineteenth century. The efforts of Eliot (1604–1690) and Brainerd (1718–1747) among the Indians of New England, the work of Ziegenbalg in translating the Scriptures into Tamil in India (New Testament in 1714), the endeavors of the Danes Hans and Paul Egede in Greenland (1722–1736), and the missionary thrust of the Moravians under Count von Zinzendorf laid the foundation for what came to be known as "the Modern Protestant Missionary Movement." This was launched, it is conventionally agreed, by the publication in 1792 of William Carey's *Enquiry into the Obligation of Christians to Use Means for the Conversion of the Heathens*, followed by his own move to India and his extraordinary efforts to see the Bible translated into a host of Indian languages. He also did yeoman work in making Indian cultures and religions and their literatures known in the West. An army of others followed in his train, bringing the gospel by the end of the period (conventionally set in 1910, date of a Missionary Conference in Edinburgh) to all but the most inaccessible parts of the earth. For this reason, Latourette called the period between 1792 and 1910 "The Great Century" of missions, and devoted three volumes— half of his *magnum opus*—to it (1970).

In the same century, Roman Catholic missions also experienced a powerful renewal. A number of new missionary orders were founded in Europe and then in the

United States, and the expansion of the church progressed apace (see Dries 1998).

Missions and Missiological Theory

But, as Wilbert Shenk has shown (1996), "mission theory" in a "scientific" sense did not always keep pace with missionary efforts. Shenk provides a masterful sketch of the beginnings of modern missiology, beginning with the development of Indigenous Church Theory by Henry Venn and Rufus Anderson in the middle third of the nineteenth century; then came the efforts of two Germans, the Lutheran Gustav Warneck and the Roman Catholic Josef Schmidlin, to place missiology on a "scientific" (*wissenschaftlich*) basis. Shenk points out that all missionary and missiological efforts from the mid–nineteenth century to the mid–twentieth were heavily influenced by the dominant scientific models, "Newtonian physics and Darwinian natural history"; and that although missions worked primarily in societies with vitalistic worldviews, Western missiology worked within a quite mechanistic worldview. This led to cultural clashes between missionaries and local peoples that were seldom fully understood by the former. To the extent that missiology interacted at all with the infant social sciences, missiology was the passive partner, absorbing ideas quite uncritically. Missions and missiology tended to place themselves quite comfortably within the colonial system and then adapted rather superficially to the era of Third-World independence after World War II. Missiology in this period was also quite church centered. But from the mid–twentieth century, this focus was sharply criticized, and emphasis began to be placed on mission as *Missio Dei*, the initiative of God operating according to God's intentions and using God's power and, if one can so speak, God's methods. Throughout, mission theory tended to shift its focus from concept to concept, one might almost say from fad to fad, without engaging the fundamental issues in a realistic manner.

This has, it would seem, improved since the 1950s. But Shenk points out that the thirteen paradigms listed by Bosch (1991) for the contemporary period seem simply to coexist in a cacophony of voices, with no serious candidate for supremacy. Ironically, the fallout of the decline of modernity has been disarray in both missiology and the social sciences.

Nevertheless, whether the missiological theory is explicit or merely implicit, every missionary effort springs from some understanding of the nature and purpose of mission. Bosch has magisterially described a succession of mission paradigms from New Testament times to the present; and he has, as I have just pointed out, listed thirteen that vie for our attention in this anarchic present time. It is not my purpose to summarize his work, nor to list the paradigms he identifies, still less to replace his model with my own. I intend only to identify certain components of some of these paradigms that are relevant to my purpose, which has to do with the relationship of missiology (latent or overt) to the social sciences (latent or overt). In other words, I will focus on the views of humankind, the human condition, and human destiny that these missiological paradigms presuppose or express. And I will emphasize more those features that the various paradigms share in common than those in which they differ, though I will also mention some of the important differentia. I also point out that, in the absence of missiology formally recognized, the features discussed derive from the theology that was current at the time and place; though in not a few instances, the persons who did mission were not highly sophisticated theologically.

So what are human beings? How did they come to be? Are they good, bad, or both, or neither? If they are good, how can we account for evil in the world? If they are bad, how can we account for good in the world? Or are human beings so determined, either by genes or by environment, that it is inappropriate to speak of good or bad? If they are bad, is there any way out for them? Do they have any destiny other than to die and disappear? Further, are human beings primarily individuals and secondarily related to groups, or are they primarily members of groups and secondarily individuals?

Missiological positions with regard to humankind and the human condition are almost invariably self-consciously derived from the Bible. But the process of interpreting the Bible, as many have pointed out, is conditioned by the cultural context of the interpreters. More, the various views expressed in the Bible are themselves not totally independent of the cultures of their respective times and places. As a result, missiological paradigms have not displayed perfect unanimity in interpreting the biblical data regarding humankind, its origin, its current condition, and its destiny. But virtually all the missiological paradigms agree that humankind has its fundamental nature from having been created "in the image and likeness of God" (Gen 1:26–27). This unique characteristic distinguishes humans from all other creatures, however closely similar they may be biologically to certain other creatures. The image of God, the consensus agrees, includes at the very least rationality, articulateness, moral discernment, relationality, imagination, creativity, and responsible authority over the rest of creation. The fact that one or other of these capacities has been in history distorted or exaggerated at the expense of the others in no degree diminishes the crucial reality and importance of each. We will see in Chapter 5 that contemporary efforts to blur or diminish the distance between humans and the rest of creation, whether for the quite legitimate purpose of defending nature from human depredations or for the quite illegitimate purpose of rejecting accountability to God, turn out to have catastrophic consequences.

The biblical picture makes it clear, in the descriptions of creation and descent from a single ancestral couple (Gen

1–2; see also Rom 5), that humanity is one "kind." Whether one takes the creation accounts literally or figuratively, the implication is the same: we are, all of us, related as members of a single species (in the scientific account that we will examine in the next chapter, this becomes an important issue). The biblical story of differentiation and separation (Gen 10–11) suggests that God's judgment upon the Tower of Babel enterprise was a redemptive judgment, relativizing what we today call culture as well as language. Sinful humans have usually made difference between groups an occasion for mutual contempt, fear, hatred, and conflict as far back as the story of Cain and Abel (Gen 4), which can be seen as representing the age-old tensions between pastoralists and agriculturalists wherever they have encountered each other. But the story of Pentecost (Acts 2) does *not* simply reverse the effects of the judgment at Babel, for different languages were not eliminated but *used* for the communication of the gospel. Henceforth, diversity is not a curse but a blessing that will be given full expression in the coming Rule of God (Rev 5:9–10).

Most missiological paradigms also understand that there has been a disastrous break between God and humankind, an alienation that has traditionally been called the Fall (Gen 3–4) and has consisted in a deliberate disobedience and rebellion of humans against God. Different missiological paradigms propose what we might call different degrees of destructiveness of the Fall. Some, following Augustine, his disciples Luther and Calvin, and most recently Barth, consider that the Fall virtually destroyed all capacity for good in human beings ("Total Depravity"), and that this radical inability for good has been automatically transmitted through human generations from parent to child, all the way back to Adam and Eve ("Original Sin"). In such a situation, even the faith by which God's grace is appropriated must be given by God, because humans are incapable of it. Others, following Pelagius and later Arminius, Wesley, Thomas Campbell, and Alexander Campbell, argue that human beings are indeed sinful and in need of salvation, but that they are capable, because of the residual image of God, of understanding and responding positively to the gospel. (I do not mean that all the persons named on either side agreed on everything, only on the one point I am making.) But all missiological paradigms agree that humans need to be saved from the ultimately disastrous consequences of their sin, that they cannot save themselves by their own efforts. Otherwise there would be no need for mission.

Missiological paradigms are also unanimous that the salvation needed has been provided by God in Jesus Christ, his unique Son. But there has been disagreement about the exact nature of this salvation (i.e., there have been a variety of "theories of the atonement"), based ultimately on emphasizing one or another of the various biblical images describing it. But the best strategy, it seems to me, is not to treat the numerous biblical images as contrasting technical terms, as has been too often done in theology, but to see them as metaphors, as complementary and often overlapping perspectives, as windows giving a view into the comprehensive mystery of God's grace from a variety of angles. In the New Testament, one dominant image, especially in the Synoptic Gospels, is that of the kingdom of God, ultimately to be restored over the entire creation, but making its initial appearance with Jesus and his followers. This image provides a comprehensive view of God's salvation that is entirely appropriate, for it was the rejection of God's rule that got us into trouble in the first place. The kingdom perspective includes both individual and corporate salvation, personal and cosmic restoration to God.

Missiological paradigms also differ in their understanding of the scope of the salvation God offers in Jesus Christ. Some argue that few will be saved; some argue for many;

some insist that in the end all will be saved (universalism). Each of these positions is founded on one or more biblical passages, usually taken out of context and in disregard of contrasting passages. Some insist that only those persons who explicitly acknowledge Jesus Christ as Lord and Savior will be saved, so that people who have never heard of him are automatically lost. (This is sometimes said to be the sole adequate motivation for Christians to become involved in mission; stories abound in missionary writings of how this position, sometimes grasped in a vision or dream, led this or that person to become a missionary.) Others argue that people cannot be held responsible for what they do not know, and that only those who have explicitly rejected Jesus Christ will be lost. Others still are convinced that non-Christians will be saved via their alternative religions. And there are numerous variations on all of these themes. Might it not be the part of prudence to allow God to decide who is "in" and who is "out"? Are not the wonder of the gospel and the command of Jesus Christ sufficient motivations for mission, without demanding that our personal intervention be the only thing that could save people from going to hell?

There is yet another dimension in which views of salvation differ, and that is the question of individual versus corporate salvation. To a certain extent, this disagreement, like the ones mentioned above, arises because there are tensions within the biblical materials themselves as well as in the cultural conditioning of its interpreters. Thus, the Old Testament offers in general a highly corporate understanding of the nature of humankind in such concepts as collective sin and guilt and collective salvation (Josh 7), but also hints at times at a somewhat more individual view (e.g., "The person who sins shall die," Ezek 18:20). The New Testament points a bit more clearly in the direction of individual differentiation (Gal 6:5), but also expresses strong communal ideas, as in the "body" language of 1

Corinthians 12 and in the cases of household salvation (Acts 16:15, 31–34). In the modern era, Church Growth Theory has made much of the pointers to group or communal response and salvation as being more appropriate in large parts of the world than purely individual appeals and incorporations into the church. The Holy Ghost missionary to Tanzania Vincent Donovan has also made the same point (1982).

The process of making salvation exclusively an individual matter, a matter of persons being rescued one by one from a future in hell for a future in heaven, began fairly early. Augustine contributed, as did the early shift from an emphasis on the coming kingdom of God to an identification of the empirical church with the kingdom as its perfect present manifestation, and the consequent refocusing of eschatology on death, judgment, heaven, and hell, rather than on the coming kingdom of God. But in the West, this tendency has grown enormously under the impact of modern individualism. This has heavily influenced both the Modern Protestant Missionary Movement and Western understandings of evangelism, especially in conservative evangelical circles. The vision is persistent that evangelism and mission consist essentially in rescuing individuals, one by one, from going to hell.

Alongside their views of what it means to be human, missiologies also have, explicitly or implicitly, views of what society and culture are like—views both of the "real" state of these things and of their ideal or potential states. For instance, during the medieval period, the church as well as the secular powers and people in general took it for granted that the existing feudal order was given of God and therefore immutable. The Enlightenment moved from that view to the opposite one that institutions were human creations and therefore subject to human alteration or replacement; and the church, *grosso modo*, moved in step with the secular world.

All of this is to say that the church, and consequently its missiologies, is deeply affected by the prevalent *Zeitgeist* of any period of history. Missions and missiology have usually adjusted themselves quite comfortably in each era not only to the prevalent worldview but also to the specific institutional and structural arrangements and the distribution and use of power that were in place. In one sense, if it were not so, there would be no occasion for the multiplicity of paradigms. This can be seen quite sharply in the diverse ways missiologies have interacted with cultures respecting the role of women. Here at times the church has been an enlightened leader that culture has followed, but too often missiology has tamely reflected the prevalent cultural patterns. In the nineteenth century, as Dana Robert has shown (1996), pioneer missions allowed women to do all kinds of things that were restricted to men back in the sending countries: preaching, teaching, baptizing converts, establishing and leading churches, administering the Eucharist. But as soon as the situation was ecclesiastically "regularized," women missionaries were once again relegated to auxiliary roles. During the same period, a number of the less sacramental denominations in the United States ordained women to the ministry in the latter part of the nineteenth century and the early twentieth; but most of them retreated from this initiative sometime in the 1930s and 1940s.

Missionary Anthropology

But it was not so much in mission theory that missionaries made their contribution in this period, as in their writings about the peoples among whom they worked. After all, of all Westerners, missionaries were the ones who had the most extensive and intensive contact with the greatest variety of exotic human groups in all continents. Just as the missionaries of the Iberian expansion of the sixteenth and seventeenth centuries encountered the literate cultures of

South and East Asia and the diverse nonliterate cultures of the New World, so the nineteenth- and twentieth-century missionaries encountered a wide range of nonliterate African and Pacific cultures. They naturally reported on what they found, both to promote their missions among the churches back home and also, increasingly, to expand knowledge in the West of these societies. As I have shown elsewhere (Taber 1991:71–72), the first reports were often bitterly negative, reflecting the personal pain the missionaries experienced through culture shock, loneliness, and sickness, as well as their naively arrogant ethnocentrism and their theological predispositions. Some missionaries provided data by correspondence to the armchair anthropologists in Europe and America. But before long, missionaries were writing once again, as had those of the sixteenth and seventeenth centuries, perceptive and sympathetic ethnographies. Names such as Codrington (1891), Junod (1927), Schmidt (1939), and Leenhardt (1979) are only the most prominent of a fairly numerous company of persons who could with complete truthfulness be called "missionary anthropologists." Some of these have justified this label further by making contributions in ways large and small to anthropological theory, such as Codrington's Melanesian concept of *mana* and of course the major contribution of Schmidt to diffusionist theory.

One must not neglect at this point to mention with appreciation the enormous contribution of missionaries to anthropological linguistics, the study of exotic languages in the contexts of their cultures. Most of the vocabularies and grammars of such languages that appeared in the nineteenth century, and a great many in the twentieth, were produced by missionaries who had the great advantage over secular anthropologists and linguists of living and interacting with the peoples they served over decades rather than months or years. Admittedly, not all of these works were highly sophisticated. But, especially since the 1930s and under the tutelage of such giants in the field as Kenneth L. Pike and Eugene A. Nida, missionary linguists have not had to apologize to anyone about the quality of their work.

Missionary Practice

Because many of the missiological convictions I have so briefly summarized were seldom formulated in any systematic way, one is obliged to discover them either by consulting informal writings, such as letters, diaries, reports to the home base, promotional literature, and the like, or from missionary practice itself. Missionary practice in the modern era, since the sixteenth century, has consisted largely in the sending of missionaries from the countries of Western Christendom to the non-Western, "pagan," or "heathen" world.

A central feature of modern missions from the beginning, both in its theological self-understanding and in its practice, was evangelism, which was understood to mean preaching the gospel and trying to persuade people to convert and to trust Jesus Christ as Lord and Savior. It is probably safe to say that apart from that passionate concern, the modern missionary enterprise would not have gotten off the ground. Everything else was secondary and auxiliary. This practice reflected, of course, the conviction that without faith in Jesus Christ, people are lost and destined for hell. Toward the end of the nineteenth century, as we will see in considering relations between missions and "the religions," this conviction suffered, among the mainline denominations, a major dilution. Correspondingly, evangelism began to take a back seat to other forms of ministry, especially social services. This in turn led to a polarization in the missionary world, especially in the United States, between those who insisted on the primacy of evangelism and those who insisted on the primacy of social services. But this polarization was a needless, and late, development; it was not so at the beginning.

For, simultaneously with the emergence of the modern missionary movement, the Western world was entering into a period of immense and unprecedented growth in wealth, power, and technical sophistication; and the non-Western world, not accidentally, was entering into a period of vast impoverishment and subjugation. As a result, missions and missionaries found themselves for the first time in history increasingly richer and more powerful than the peoples they addressed. This fact created enormous problems for the communication of the gospel, problems that were rarely detected by missionaries. Bonk (1991) has dealt masterfully with the economic dimensions of the difficulty; but the discrepancies in wealth and power also greatly aggravated cultural misunderstandings.

Among other things, the affluence, power, and cultural sophistication of the missionaries led to an overemphasis on what the local people *did not* have: not only were they materially poor, but they were judged to be intellectually, morally, and esthetically destitute—benighted. They were, it is true, in most cases illiterate; for even in the great literate Asian cultures, the lower-class or lower-caste masses of the populations, which were more accessible to the missionaries than the educated elites, were illiterate. So mission came, in its ruthless benevolence, to supply this bottomless *lack*. It did not help, of course, that many features of the local cultures, such as nudity, drumming, "lascivious" dancing, "crude" carving, polygamy, and so forth, offended the missionaries' Western sensibilities and Western interpretations of Christian morality. Lacking any sense of the relative coherence and integration of culture, the missionaries tended to attack specific cultural features without regard to how these fit into larger patterns or even to what these features meant at a deeper level. And they insisted, out of the riches of their cultural capital, that the forbidden offending customs be replaced with "Christian," that is, Western, ones. Such was the combination of Western generosity and arrogance that gave rise to the charge of "cultural imperialism," a charge that is to varying degrees true, but is not, as Lamin Sanneh has rightly insisted, the whole story (Sanneh 1990).

Fairly early in this process, then, the pattern was established that missionaries, being increasingly the "haves" in the equation, were obligated to provide for the "have-nots" they were addressing not only the gospel but also the financial and technical good things offered by their cultures. A combination of factors led to this view, factors that were expressed in various proportions by different missions: first, a perhaps rather dim recollection of the comprehensive nature of Jesus' own ministry to lost and needy people; then a sincere pity and compassion for the destitute and "benighted" peoples they encountered; finally, an increasingly confident and even arrogant sense of the superiority of their "Christian" culture and its benefits, which they were eager to share with those who did not have them. The resulting conviction led to what much later came to be called a "comprehensive" mission strategy. This almost always included education and medicine, initially in fairly rudimentary fashion; then, as missions became more and more affluent, it led to huge institutions: colleges, universities, and fully-equipped hospitals. Fairly often, the comprehensive approach included agricultural and industrial training and projects, economic development projects, and community development projects. These last sometimes took the form of separate "Christian" communities, such as the Jesuit *reducciones* in Latin America.

Various formal justifications were given for these enterprises: some argued that these worldly benefits were part and parcel of the gospel; some insisted that they could be justified only if they were used as a tactic to win a hearing for the gospel, narrowly understood; others said that the social services were a fruit of the gospel; and finally some said that evangelism and social assistance constituted two distinct but legitimate expressions of Christian mission. The irony is that whatever the official rationale, there was always a great danger that people would see the material benefits to be reaped by associating with missionaries and "convert" for those benefits rather than because of the intrinsic validity and persuasiveness of the gospel. In fact, the term *rice Christians* was coined in China in the nineteenth century to designate just such persons. Competing religions have also not been slow to see in the social services of missions an inducement to convert; Muslims deeply resent this understanding, and the State of Israel has enacted rigorous laws to prevent this from happening. On the other hand, when missions have refrained from providing social services, they have sometimes been accused of lack of compassion.

One problem was that the services missions did provide took forms suggested by the fact that missionaries had plenty of money and technology, and simply followed models from their home countries in founding hospitals, schools, and other institutions. These were inevitably highly foreign to the local scene and vastly beyond the means of local churches, so that long after these churches achieved independence in the wake of the political independence of their countries, they were not able to support and control the institutions.

The situation was greatly aggravated for many American missions, as I mentioned above, when American Protestantism dichotomized into "modernist" and "fundamentalist" camps, with the former committing themselves to the "social gospel" and the latter, in reaction, eschewing social services and restricting themselves to preaching the gospel and planting churches. As a matter of fact, the self-restriction was never absolute: many conservative missions did operate educational and medical programs, though sometimes with a bad conscience and usually under the rationalization that these were the means to evangelism. The polarization seems not to have taken such a radical form in Europe.

Missions and Governments

The history of relations between church and state since the first century is exceedingly complex and tangled. At the risk of oversimplification, the church has at different times been (a) an ignored, then despised, then persecuted minority in the Roman Empire; (b) in the fourth century, tolerated, then established as the religious arm of the Roman state, falling into the same pattern as the previous civic pagan religions; (c) midwife, after the collapse of the western Empire, to a new political synthesis, culminating in the Holy Roman Empire (early ninth century); (d) a state among other states, today known as Vatican City; (e) established as an institution of the state, following several different patterns in various European countries; (f) a "free," separate institution, or complex of institutions, as in many countries to this day. The theological/philosophical positions taken by the spokespersons for the church are also varied: (a) through the Middle Ages, the church saw itself as a kind of *primus inter pares* state among the emerging states of Europe; (b) Luther argued that there were two parallel kingdoms, the church, representing the kingdom of God, and the state, representing the secular realm (this position has at times been applied in a quite categorical way to argue that the church should never interfere in matters of state); (c) Calvin saw the church as separate from the state, but serving as the conscience of the state; (d) Anabaptists saw the church as existing over against the state as an alternative society, and involved in the state in only a highly selective manner; (e) today, some, including some Anabaptists and the French thinker Jacques Ellul (1991), argue for anarchy—but in a specific sense: that the

church ought to radically *relativize* the state and its structures and processes, *demythologizing* its absolutist pretensions and participating (e.g., as citizens) only insofar as
participation is not in conflict with the prior claims of the
kingdom of God.

In modern cross-cultural missions, relations with governments have varied greatly. Some missions and missionaries applied the dichotomous view of the world, Christian
versus non-Christian, to the governments involved; that is,
governments of countries in Christendom were Christian
and therefore to be obeyed; governments in heathendom
were heathen and therefore to be defied if they offered any
resistance to the gospel. Many others took a variety of more
nuanced views, depending on what their particular theologies did with Romans 13 and related passages in the New
Testament.

The picture was—and is—greatly complicated by the
fact that for the majority of missionaries in the modern
movement, at least two governments were/are involved:
the government of the missionary's home country and the
local (communal) government. For many, a third government was involved—the colonial, alternatively the national,
government, when this was different from that of the missionary's home country. In other words, an American missionary in a French colony, as I was, had to deal with three
authorities. The government of the United States, in my
case, played no role other than to issue my passport,
though, as we will see, issues of loyalty to this government
might arise. But the French government had to issue me a
visa to permit me to reside and work in their colony, and
they felt free to set very specific conditions on my admittance and continued residence in the colony. And, once on
the spot, I had, to some extent, to deal with the very local
but very real "traditional" authority, which the colonial
system had left in place in highly modified form for its own
purposes. Other missions experienced variations on this

theme. The Summer Institute of Linguistics (SIL), for instance, has been bitterly criticized in some quarters for its high-profile cordial relations with national governments that are not always perceived to be—and often are not—working for the good of the tribal populations that SIL serves in the field. It is also the case that the situation has altered substantially since independence in many former colonies. Quite a few countries remain hospitable to the church and to the gospel without finding it necessary to admit many foreign missionaries; the argument is that there are plenty of national Christians to do all that needs to be done, and that foreigners are therefore superfluous. Other countries have become decidedly less open to the gospel, and some have even begun persecuting churches and Christians.

A perennial temptation for missionaries has been to forget that they are guests in the country of residence, and therefore admitted on sufferance; they sometimes tend to expect or even demand "rights" that as foreigners they do not have.

It is my observation and general impression that on the whole, missions have tended to be pragmatic rather than ideological (or theological!) in their relations with governments of all kinds. But on occasion, they have taken decided stands that, however, do not reflect any kind of consistent pattern. For instance, in the conflicts between traditional rulers and aspiring colonial powers, some missionaries defended the traditional authorities; some took the side of the colonial system. In general, throughout the nineteenth and early twentieth centuries, missionaries became increasingly positive about, and even committed to, the colonial system. In the post–World War II era of confrontations leading to independence, missionaries again took various positions. In a few highly violent situations, as in Zimbabwe (formerly Rhodesia), there were missionaries on both sides of the conflict, as well as some who tried desperately to straddle the fence and even a few who tried to be peacemakers. In other words, it is hard to discover a principled position, let alone a consistent one, on this question.

On the whole, missionaries have tended either to defend the policies and actions of their home governments or to remain silent about them. I have actually heard a missionary say, at a missionary convention in the United States, that "the United States in its relations with other countries has always acted in love." In another instance, when I pointed out to a group of missionaries the nefarious role the United States had played in the decline of the economies of several of the Third-World countries in which they worked, they rejected my interpretation vehemently and insisted that the problems were entirely the fault of the national governments. This leads me to remark that missions that expressed great respect and appreciation for their home governments and for colonial governments (often appealing to Rom 13) did not always show the same respect for national or local authorities. They forgot, in other words, that the government that Paul was referring to in this chapter was a very pagan and corrupt one, the Roman Empire of Nero. In the 1860s, for example, Roman Catholic missions appealed to the French navy to force open the doors of Vietnam for their work. American Protestant missions were virtually unanimous in support of America's conquest of the Philippines in 1898, seeing it as a way of furthering their efforts. In the nineteenth century, many Western missions working in China demanded and obtained, under pressure from their home governments, "extraterritoriality," that is, immunity from the authority of the Chinese government. This, by the way, was sometimes extended to their converts, which was a not inconsiderable example of the benefits that appealed to "rice Christians." Later, after the Boxer Rebellion (1900), Western governments by threat of military attack forced the Chinese government to pay damages to missions for the depredations of the rebels; only the China Inland

Mission, to its great honor, refused the damages. More recently, several American missions took great pride in defying the laws of eastern European countries by smuggling Bibles into those countries, thus tweaking the nose of "godless communism." Ironically, during that same period, the United Bible Societies imported into those same countries, quite legally, many times the number of Bibles imported by all the smugglers combined. Finally, during the Vietnam War, American missionaries routinely accepted rides in American military aircraft as the best way to get around the country, a tactic that led later to reprisals against Vietnamese Christians when the missionaries were gone.

This discussion of the relations of missions to governments is intended to illustrate the dangers of naivete in dealing with political power, and its uses and abuses—a naivete that missionaries shared with most of their fellow Christians in their home countries. Might missions have been better served by taking heed to the more sophisticated perspectives of the social sciences? On the other hand, social scientists turn out not to be unanimous, nor even always very insightful, in dealing with these issues!

Missions and "the Religions"

Relations of missionaries with the religions they have found where they have worked have historically been rather hostile and even stormy. Confrontation was the rule, for missionaries were convinced that these religions were demonic and that their devotees were going to hell unless they converted to Christianity. This exclusivist position continues to hold sway over many missionaries and missiologists; it is even argued that if this were not the case, if perchance the religions might play some positive or even salvific role for its practitioners, then Christian mission would be totally superfluous. Hence, the exclusivist position was deemed to be necessary to the apologetic for mission.

This began to change for at least some Christians in the nineteenth century. At the 1893 Parliament of Religions in Chicago, for instance, under the charismatic influence of Vivekananda of India, a strong pressure for religious egalitarianism and relativism swept the assembly and was expressed in its reports. World War I and its demoralizing impact on the West added to the loss of conviction in the Western missionary movement, finding expression, for instance, in the *Report of the Laymen's Enquiry on Re-Thinking Missions* (1932), edited by W. E. Hocking of Harvard. Since then, Christian thinking about "the religions" has gravitated around three foci: the traditional *exclusivist* position, which continues dominant in some circles; an *inclusivist* position, epitomized by Karl Rahner's attempt to include people of other religions in salvation as "anonymous Christians" (an effort that won no thanks from those people!); and a radically *pluralist* (or *relativist*) position, best expressed by John Hick (1977) and Paul Knitter (1985), that rejects the universal necessity of faith in Christ and insists that everyone will be saved through his or her own religion, because all religions have at bottom the same object of worship and the same ultimate values and goals. Others, notably DiNoia (1992) and Heim (1995), point out that these assertions are in fact simply not true, and that the profound differences between the religions in both starting points and ultimate goals must be taken seriously into account. The Hick/Knitter position, like the Rahner position, turns out in fact to be both very Western and quite ruthlessly totalitarian. In any case, the tripartite model is itself far too rigid to account for the extraordinary diversity of positions that have flourished in this century.

Nevertheless, this debate has had the net effect of cutting the nerve of missionary motivation for many people in Western churches and also, indirectly, of giving the body of missionaries an increasingly "conservative" personality, by default, for fewer and fewer people in the "liberal" denominations are interested.

Summary

With respect to other institutions and facilities of the modern West, missionaries seem simply to have taken them for granted as good: banking, facilities for travel and communications, technology—all were simply absorbed uncritically as means made available, by God's goodness, to facilitate mission.

Some missions, notably the Basel Mission in West Africa, established commercial enterprises that originally functioned as both a commissariat for missionaries and a place of training and employment for nationals. The Basel Mission's enterprise, in fact, became so successful that, spun off from the mission as an independent trading company, it came to be one of the biggest businesses in today's Ghana. Similarly, the American Presbyterian Mission in Cameroun founded an industrial training program that manufactured furniture sold throughout that part of Africa.

So missionary practice has been extremely diverse, reflecting a combination of theological/missiological conviction; beliefs, attitudes, and values from their home cultures; and pragmatic considerations on the local scene, often seen in a relatively short-term perspective. This *pragmatism* of mission deserves to be underlined. As one might expect of a missiology partly shaped by the modern outlook, it easily thinks and talks in terms of cause-and-effect, of problems and solutions, and—continually—of methods and means, of tools and techniques. This can be seen from the opening gun: the term *means* is conspicuous in the title of William Carey's 1792 *Enquiry*. Today, the most fiercely pragmatic missiology is that which goes under the label Church Growth. The fascinating thing is that, as Church Growth Theory has declined slightly in cross-cultural missionary circles, it has been picked up by administrators in mainline denominations in the United States who are in a panic about their serious and continuous loss of members over recent decades.

I should not be read as condemning pragmatism per se. There is no virtue in working haphazardly or ineffectually. Pragmatism becomes problematic only when it rejects the conditions placed upon its operations by the nature of the gospel, as when manipulative or coercive means are used to proclaim what is innately a liberating gospel. In such cases, the focus on *means* can all too readily occasion a shift in the nature of the ends envisaged.

3

The Social Sciences

Meanwhile, social philosophers in the West were continuing to develop new ideas about society and culture on foundations laid by the Enlightenment. As these ideas gained elaboration and acceptance, and the physical sciences made huge strides in theory, method, and findings, the proponents of these ideas began to think of themselves as scientists and their systems of ideas as sciences on the model of the physical sciences. Gradually, several formal disciplines arose: anthropology, sociology, psychology, political science, economics. It is not easy to justify in a fully logical way the distinctions between these disciplines. Anthropology and sociology are natural cousins. They differ primarily because in the early division of labor sociology focused on modern Western societies and anthropology focused on the small, exotic societies of the world. Political science is, in the eyes of a few at least (Minogue 1995), rather arbitrarily separated from sociology in dealing with the special area of the use of power for social control and coordination. But political science has in fact borrowed much more heavily from economics and psychology for its conceptual foundations. Economics has tended to cut itself off from the others by insisting on the autonomy of the market and the rigor claimed for its methods. But if Jane

Collier is right (1992), economics as an ideology (which she calls economism) is increasingly claiming sovereignty over all of life. Psychology, of course, works primarily with individuals and invests heavily in its therapeutic intent. Once the boundaries were established, however arbitrarily, each discipline developed its official historiography, but all rest on conceptual foundations and perpetuate debates from at least two centuries and more earlier. For instance, already before and during the Enlightenment, information or pseudo-information about exotic societies fed into this process. Introductory textbooks for undergraduates tend to present a highly sanitized, falsely harmonized view of the disciplines, no doubt in order to make them attractive to students. But they are in fact in some disarray. Few if any concepts, even major ones, are universally accepted within any one discipline, and tensions between the disciplines are rife.

One of the giants of the nineteenth century who contributed mightily to the development of economics, political science, and sociology/anthropology, and more generally to the philosophic underpinnings of all the emergent social sciences, was Karl Marx (1818–1883). His many writings, including *The Communist Manifesto* (1848) and *Das Kapital* (Ncl. trans. 1887), laid out both an analysis of European society and a program for the eventual "scientific" revolution that would eliminate exploitation and alienation and usher in the communistic, or classless, society. Marx epitomizes the tension in the social sciences we will discuss later between a rigorous ("scientific") determinism and a vigorous messianic utopianism. Though few if any of the other nineteenth-century founders of the social sciences were directly influenced by Marx, concepts that he developed became increasingly influential in the twentieth century. He himself, by the way, was heavily influenced by the evolutionary scheme of the American anthropologist Lewis Henry Morgan.

Let us now examine each of the social sciences in turn, focusing on basic ideas and dominant personalities. We will see that sociology and anthropology arose from the same philosophical roots, but soon diverged, first in their subject matter, then in their methods. Sociology paid attention primarily to modern, complex societies, the societies of which its practitioners were themselves members, whereas anthropology studied exotic, often nonliterate societies in which its practitioners were total foreigners. This difference in focus led before long to a considerable difference in methods. Political science was built on the conceptual foundations laid by the political philosophers already mentioned—Machiavelli, Locke, Rousseau, and their like. Economics was based on the writings of Adam Smith, David Ricardo, John Stuart Mill, Thomas Malthus, and a number of others, including, in a few cases, Karl Marx. Psychology, for its part, had its birth in the medical attempt to deal with mental and emotional disorders.

Sociology

Sociology aims to study societies, social groups, social institutions, and social processes, almost exclusively in the investigator's own society. Being a member, the investigator starts out with the assumption of a high level of personal knowledge and understanding of how things work, and tries to refine and deepen that knowledge and understanding. But the sociologist must make special efforts to counteract the power of his or her internalized, socially generated biases. One significant feature of sociology is that the units of study, which are social groups, are in a real sense empirically available to observation; this fact establishes a contrast with the anthropological concept of "culture," which is not empirically available.

The decisive step in putting the study of human and social phenomena on a "scientific" basis was taken by the Frenchman Auguste Comte (1798–1857), who coined the term *sociology* as the label for the "science of society" (1839) and wrote voluminously through the 1850s. Comte developed a sociology that was first of all *evolutionary* in that it postulated three stages in the inevitable progress of human styles of thought throughout history: the theological or mythological (superstitious) style of "primitives"; the metaphysical (speculative) style of the ancient Greeks; and the positive (scientific) style, this last being essentially Comte's own contribution. Second, it was *utopian* in that it envisaged a secular *eschaton* that would be the ideal society in which the official religion would be the religion of Humanity, consciously designed by Comte himself for maximum social utility. It should be mentioned that he had absolutely no use for a religion based on revelation or a religion bearing authority. Finally, it was *evangelistic* in that it aspired by vigorous propagation to supplant all alternative social arrangements by a design based (at last) on rigorous scientific premises.

In the second half of the nineteenth century, Herbert Spencer (1820–1903) continued the work of Comte and propounded the concept of what was later called "social Darwinism" to describe what he conceived of as the inevitable and necessary struggle between peoples and populations, so that the "fittest" would survive and dominate. In other words, Spencer's "program" for the betterment of humanity was to allow the struggle for survival, unhindered in any way, to weed out and/or subjugate the lesser peoples and to bring the superior peoples to the top of the pile. This was a popular ideological support for colonialism and high imperialism, which reached their height soon after the work of Spencer.

Early in the twentieth century, however, social evolutionism began to be discredited by a growing body of contradictory empirical evidence. (Obviously, this should not be taken to mean the eclipse of biological evolution, which continues to dominate all fields of biology, including human biology, to this day.) I will say more about this in discussing anthropology. But the French scholar Durkheim (1858–1917) developed in its place as the central focus of sociology the concept of social *function*, and argued that this, rather than historical origins or development, was in any case the crucial subject matter for sociology. The various institutions of a society, he insisted, functioned in an integrated complex of mutually supportive ways to sustain the society. All customs, all systems, all institutions could thus be explained in terms of their functions in maintaining the well-being of society and its members. Religion, for instance, existed to provide a necessary sacred legitimation and sanction to bring all members of society into compliance for the good of society as a whole. If at any time the system broke down, so that some or all of the parts of the social structure no longer functioned adequately, a period of *anomie* ensued—that is, a period without norms in which people no longer knew how to live or what to do. Krass (1978:51–60) has argued that Durkheim saw in *anomie* a moment not only of crisis but of opportunity for novel and more effective patterns to emerge. For this reason, Krass calls Durkheim's sociology "less a sociology of what is than a sociology of what is becoming." In this way, if Krass is right, Durkheim could be considered to be a modified utopian.

But the net influence of Durkheim, especially via such interpreters as Talcott Parsons in the United States, was to create very much a "sociology of what is." The mentality that prevailed under structural functionalism was that if something worked, its existence was *ipso facto* justified. One might summarize this attitude with respect to society by means of the popular American saying: "If it ain't broke, don't fix it." Incidentally, the same influence, mediated by the British anthropologists Radcliffe-Brown (1922) and Malinowski (1922), created an "anthropology of what is." In anthropology, this manner of thinking was reinforced by the strong emphasis on cultural relativism that came to prevail.

One more major figure in sociology deserves mention, if only because he was one of the few scholars of his time to work in terms of an overarching conceptual scheme, in what might be called macrosociology—the German Max Weber. His *The Protestant Ethic and the Spirit of Capitalism* (Ncl. trans. 1947) attempted to show causal connections between these major historical realities. Later, such world-system and world-systems theorists as Wallerstein and Braudel have revived the use of macroschemes (see Sanderson 1995).

More recently, sociology has not only increasingly abandoned as unworkable and incompatible with scientific detachment the utopian idealism of its founders, but it has also tried to achieve rigor by tackling very small questions—what might be called microsociology—and by using statistical methods to analyze input from large numbers of subjects. But sociologists have often been insufficiently aware of how much imprecision is introduced into their studies by the ordinary-language wording of the questions they formulate, for example, in their interviews and questionnaires. Empirical data of the right sort are of course of the utmost value in all scientific endeavors, but they are not *ipso facto* significant. However, not a few social scientists seem to revel in empirical data for their own sake, important or trivial, sound or unsound, and to manipulate them endlessly, in a procedure devoid of theory, in the groundless hope that somehow reality will emerge.

One branch of sociology—the sociology of knowledge—is of special interest to us because it is concerned with epistemology, the theory of knowledge. But its treatment of knowledge differs significantly from the treatments found in philosophy, because it bases differences in knowledge and belief squarely on social realities, especially class, race, and nationality. Though it has taken a number of not fully compatible forms since its beginning early in this century, all of these forms take their origin from the suspicion of

Marx that the beliefs of persons and human groups were shaped by the position of those persons and groups in larger social structures and systems, each set of beliefs being designed to make its proponents look as good as possible. A lucid presentation of one form of the sociology of knowledge is Peter L. Berger and Thomas Luckmann's *The Social Construction of Reality* (1967). We will see later how the sociology of knowledge relates to anthropology's cultural relativity and prepares the way for the even more radical relativism of postmodernism.

I cannot leave the sociology of knowledge without mentioning briefly a discussion that has been carried on within sociology about the very nature of the discipline. I refer to the stance that describes the social sciences as hermeneutical or interpretive disciplines rather than explanatory disciplines like the physical sciences. Hekman (1986) has pointed out that the various forms of sociology of knowledge have conceptual roots going back to Dilthey and Marx, which in this century have found expression in the work of Gadamer and Mannheim. Though the different voices within sociology of knowledge clash at some points, they converge on this one—that the human scene does not lend itself to the kind of dispassionate, detached, positivist analysis, prediction, and control that characterize the physical sciences. Their more modest task is to understand (*verstehen*), to interpret, the human scene in much the same way as texts are interpreted.

Jürgen Habermas (1971, 1973) offers an even more profound critique of the variety of theories of knowledge, going back to Kant and Hegel, that have underlain the social sciences. Habermas argues that when science became completely self-reflective, it divorced itself from philosophical epistemology and created its own approach to validation by reduction, which Habermas calls "scientism" and characterizes as follows: "'Scientism' means science's belief in itself: that is the conviction that one can no longer understand science as *one* form of possible knowledge but rather must identify knowledge with science" (1971:4). He goes on to criticize Comte's positivism that grounded this move. This is the arrogant view that only science can generate real knowledge. As for Marx, Habermas points out that he was inconsistent, wavering between two opinions—that "the science of man" that he was founding was and was not a natural science. "Although he himself established the science of man in the form of critique and not as a natural science, he continually tended to classify it with the natural sciences" and invoked "the model of physics" where "the economic law of motion of modern society is the 'natural law'" understood as a law of nature (1971:45). Habermas also dealt with the contrast mentioned by Hekman, between the natural sciences as explanatory and the social sciences as interpretive; he founds his discussion on several thinkers, including Dilthey.

Hekman, for her part, goes on to elaborate on the final conclusion of this process—what some would call its *reductio ad absurdum*—in postmodernism (Foucault) and deconstruction, which she calls respectively "moral nihilism" and "conceptual nihilism" (1986:171–96). In this, she agrees with Milbank.

Anthropology

Anthropology, alone among the social sciences, purports ambitiously—and no doubt presumptuously—to deal *holistically* with the human condition. Not only does its incarnation as cultural/social anthropology study the cultures, social structures, and technologies of many peoples around the world, but in its other incarnations it also studies the material remains of their past, taken as circumstantial evidence (archeology); their languages (anthropological linguistics); and their physical constitution—human evolution, human genetics, and so forth—(physical/biological anthropology). The holistic nature of the discipline, which is an axiomatic part of its self-definition, is nevertheless hard to maintain in the face of the increasing complexity and specialization of each of the subdisciplines. It has been a couple of generations at least since any single anthropologist could aspire to make significant contributions to more than one of these fields. Because missionaries and missiologists have had little if anything to do with the other branches of anthropology, I will focus here largely on cultural/social anthropology and to a lesser extent on anthropological linguistics. Physical anthropology will, however, become necessary to our concerns when we discuss biological evolution. The reason, by the way, for the clumsy dual form "cultural/social" is that some anthropologists, chiefly in Great Britain, focused on social structures and in this way were closer to sociologists, whereas others, chiefly in the United States, focused on the "culture." It was no accident that the considerable influence of Durkheim in anthropology was mediated chiefly through the very British anthropologist Radcliffe-Brown. As for the term *culture*, as I have shown elsewhere (Taber 1991:45), it was first used in something akin to the present sense in German in the 1840s and in English in the 1860s. American anthropologists, especially Kroeber (1948), during one phase in the history of the discipline reified culture and assigned to it extraordinary determinative powers.

Today, it is axiomatic in all branches of anthropology that humankind is a single, highly homogeneous species, *Homo sapiens sapiens*. Diversity within this species, in skin color but also in general body size and shape, in hair texture, and in facial features, to name only the most visible human traits, is usually attributed to the pressures of environmental factors on relatively isolated gene pools, which led these gene pools to become what some still insist on calling "races." In the nineteenth century, the races of humankind were taken to be very different, discrete, and readily rankable on scales of intelligence, moral character, and cultural development, in an evolutionary sequence. This was, though not the origin of racism, the pseudo-scientific ideological ground of that terrible phenomenon that still haunts us. Some scholars until well into the present century—Coon of Harvard among them—continued to insist that the different races had distinct origins arising from different prehuman species of hominids. The contemporary understanding in physical anthropology, however, is that *Homo sapiens* originated as, and continues to be, a single species, and that the features we all have in common are far more numerous and matter far more than the external features that distinguish us. Races are now seen to be relatively unstable realities with highly permeable boundaries, unless they continue to exist in isolation from one another. But the different gene pools vary far less than, say, varieties of dogs. Most differences of behavior among humans now tend to be assigned to cultural causes, because each culture is seen to shape human beings into a particular pattern. But even culture is now under critical scrutiny.

Anthropology had its beginnings in the mid–nineteenth century. It was from the 1840s to the 1870s that Bastian in Germany, Edward B. Tylor in England (*Primitive Culture*, 1871) and Lewis Henry Morgan in the United States (*Ancient Society*, 1877), among others, developed the discipline of cultural anthropology. Given the *Zeitgeist* of the nineteenth century, as we saw in discussing sociology, anthropological theories could not have been anything but evolutionary. So Tylor argued for a universal evolution in religious ideas, beginning in "primitive" societies with the "animistic" notion that all reality was indwelt by spirit, then moving through to polytheism, and ultimately to monotheism. Primitive peoples were stuck at the first, animistic level; some few peoples had advanced to polytheism; but only the most advanced, "civilized" peoples had achieved monotheism.

Morgan, for his part, posited an evolutionary scheme, mostly in the technological domain but also partly involving social structures, which comprised three stages: savagery, barbarism, and civilization. Each was subdivided into three substages: lower, middle, and upper, based on specific cultural details. Thus, some "savages" had moved through the three phases of savagery to "barbarism," and some barbarians had finally become civilized. Specific technological or social clues—for example, archery, chieftainship—signaled the passage from stage to stage and determined which peoples were to be assigned to which pigeonholes.

All of these schemes were evolutionary; that is, they purported to study and explain how societies, cultures, and economies came to be the way they were through the inexorable working of wholly immanent properties and processes. All the stages and criteria were supposed to be universal; that is, all peoples inexorably moved from one stage to the other via the same steps in the same sequence. The only difference was that some peoples had climbed faster and farther than others. All of these schemata were in various ways quite deterministic and Procrustean, and all took it as a matter of course that the modern Western models were at the acme of the process and that all other models were destined in time to approximate the Western ones or to disappear. In this century, all of these rigid universal schemes were discredited by the mountainous accumulation of empirical data from around the world that simply refused to fit into them.

For it has been in this century that anthropology, like sociology, has also seen a strong reaction against the racism and ethnocentrism of the evolutionary schemes and has been increasingly shaped by other concepts, notably the structural functionalism of Durkheim as well as various modified versions of humanism and materialism. Anthropology also invented and pushed the idea of cultural relativism, especially in the works of Boas (1940), Kroeber (1948), Herskovits (1973), and their disciples in the United States, and Malinowski in Great Britain. Newer, nonracist evolutionary models have been proposed more recently (e.g., Steward 1955; White 1959). White, for example, attempted to explain and universalize evolution by abstracting from the particulars of each situation a calculation based on a quantification of the increasing control of energy from all sources: human and animal muscles, fire, water power, fossil fuels, nuclear fuels, solar power, and so forth. Meanwhile—especially in Europe—diffusionism was highly developed (Schmidt 1939). This is the concept that if a specific cultural feature occurs in more than one place in the world, the odds are that that feature was originally created in one place and then was borrowed in the other places of its occurrence. There have been both highly doctrinaire forms of diffusionism and milder, more empirically based forms. Marxism, both straight and modified, has influenced some. Efforts have been made to create a "humanistic" anthropology, and most recently postmodernism has had an impact, reinforcing earlier ideas of cultural relativity. But throughout the history of the discipline, and especially at the present moment, no single theoretical model has dominated the field with any degree of continuity or unanimity. Despite works like Harris's *The Rise of Anthropological Theory* (1968), anthropology has not generated any conceptual frameworks comparable to theories in the physical sciences. Harris himself is an ideologically committed historical materialist and wants desperately to make anthropology a "nomothetic" (i.e., law-formulating) science. But clearly, the only laws any of the social sciences could in principle formulate would be probabilistic generalizations.

At this point it becomes necessary to elucidate the concept of *culture*, which is the major intellectual construct in anthropology. Beginning with Tylor in 1871, culture has been defined in literally hundreds of ways (Kroeber and Kluckhohn 1952). But almost all definitions have in common a number of features, which I have elsewhere summarized as follows:

Culture is a more or less coherent set of ideas (symbols, taxonomies, definitions, explanations, values, attitudes, and rules), *which are created and shared by a group of people and transmitted to their children, and which enable them to make sense of their experience and to cope with their natural and social worlds to their collective advantage* (Taber 1991:3).

I go on (1991:4–7) to spell out certain features that enable culture to do what it is supposed to do: it is (a) learned, (b) mental, (c) adaptive, (d) shared by a group, (e) selective among options potentially available, (f) normative, incorporating rewards and penalties to ensure compliance, (g) more or less integrated, (h) heterogeneous, (i) cumulative, and (j) adaptable. This means that humans are more vulnerable even than other hominids during infancy and youth when they have not yet learned the culture, but more fully able to cope with changing and unforeseen circumstances once they have learned their culture adequately.

But more needs to be said. Culture has at some times been almost reified and assigned a quasi-omnipotence in shaping human persons and groups. This led missiology, when it became informed by anthropology, to have an exaggerated respect and even awe for the immovable nature of the cultural "rock" standing before missionaries. This was in some ways an improvement over the cavalier cultural iconoclasm that characterized some missionaries at their worst, but it undermined the sense that the gospel could and ought to change certain aspects of any culture. Cultures have also been seen, especially in the functionalist perspective of Malinowski, as discrete, closed, bounded entities, existing side by side as so many monads, each the possession of a discrete, closed, bounded set of persons called a society (societies in the "primitive" world tended to be called "tribes"). As long as a culture was functioning properly, it was seen as existing in equilibrium and therefore as avoiding change; change in such a situation would in fact be pathological, a sign of malfunction or of aggressive outside influence. This was one source of hostility toward missionaries among anthropologists. Later, it became obviously clear that, especially in the contemporary scene, cultures are at least as leaky as "races," and that contact between persons and groups of several cultures is the normal state of affairs and leads to mutual influences and changes. For that matter, it has been made clear by scholars working with various geographically and historically large-scale perspectives such as world civilizations, systems theory, and system-theory (see Sanderson 1995), that mutual cultural influences, piggybacking on trade in commodities over astonishing distances, have operated ever since the dawn of human experience. Scholars such as Fernand Braudel, Immanuel Wallerstein, and André Gunder Frank have made the case very persuasively. In world-systems theory, evolution and diffusion (especially as regards technical matters) converge into a larger picture of cumulative innovation and mutual cultural influences and exchanges.

More recently, some scholars have denigrated the concept of culture, arguing that because it is "only in people's heads" and therefore not empirically available as society is, and because it is so evidently unstable over time, it should not constitute the field of study for a science. These scholars have been influenced by postmodernism's skepticism about any such metanarrative as culture has purported to be. And even many of the scholars who continue to work with the concept of culture feel the need to qualify it, to make it much less coherent and cohesive, much less powerful, much less stable over time than their predecessors did (see Munch and Smelser 1992).

No doubt the holistic ambition of anthropology, as it emerged, contributed to the de facto bifurcation between anthropology and sociology that developed quite soon in the history of these sister disciplines. As they began to distinguish themselves from each other, it was anthropology that concerned itself with the data from the exotic places (which, coincidentally, was where most missionaries worked), especially in that part of the non-Western world that came to be called "primitive," whereas sociology focused on the complex modern societies of which its practitioners were themselves members. Because of the obvious vastness and complexity of its subject matter, sociology seldom succumbed to the common anthropological illusion of being able to provide a complete portrait of any society; but it also found itself tempted more often to be satisfied with fragmentary accounts, reductionism, and lingering ethnocentrism.

What I have just called a "common anthropological illusion" was a further manifestation of the holistic aspiration of anthropology. When a cultural/social anthropologist went into the field to spend a period of months or years in a particular small human community, it was his or her aim to bring back a complete account of the society in question. The smallness and supposed structural simplicity of the communities studied were assumed to make this breathtaking aim achievable. And so there appeared from the twenties through the sixties, in Great Britain, the United States, and in Europe, a spate of monographs giving in a few hundred pages what was purported to be a complete description of the culture/social structure of society X. A typical monograph included one or more chapters on each of the major divisions of culture: material culture, social culture, and expressive or ideational culture.

I have so far used the term *primitive* without explanation. But, because the so-called primitive world became for a long time almost the exclusive focus of anthropology, we need to elucidate it. As Kuper (1988) has shown, the notion that some societies are primitive was invented in the nineteenth century (as earlier writers had used the term *savage* to designate exotic nonliterate peoples, whether "noble" or not) to explain why these societies were so poorly developed, especially in technological matters. The term originally was meant to suggest (see the ideas of Tylor and Morgan above) that all human societies at their first beginning were alike in having few technological means at their disposal, in having only elementary social and religious ideas and structures, and the like. In other words, "primitive" had a clearly temporal meaning, supposedly going back as it did to the dawn of human experience. But from that identical beginning, different societies were supposed to have climbed the ladder of "progress" at astonishingly different rates of speed, and some peoples apparently failed to climb beyond the earliest rungs. As we have seen, the ladder was everywhere the same; it was only people who differed in their achievements or abilities in the climb. It was not hard, on this foundation, to suppose that failure to climb was due to the innate, genetic inferiority of the unsuccessful peoples; this notion was, of course, the academic form of the racism that prevailed in the Western world during the nineteenth century and continued to rule in some quarters in physical anthropology well into the present century. (It should also be said that some of the most powerful rebuttals against racism have come from other quarters in physical anthropology.) Agreeing as it did with Spencerian thinking, this evolutionary racist mode of understanding was clearly highly compatible with colonialism and imperialism, and with such popular notions of the day as "the white man's burden" (to rule, of course) and "Manifest Destiny."

Perhaps because, unlike the sociologists, anthropologists were not members of the societies they studied, and needed to establish at least a social basis from which to function, anthropology has in this century relied heavily on fieldwork, and especially on "participant observation" in the culture to be studied. More and more anthropologists entered the field in person. (The German Frobisher and the Englishman Rivers were early practitioners of anthropological fieldwork, and fieldwork became the sine qua non of professional anthropology with Boas, Malinowski, and Radcliffe-Brown.) In this method, the anthropologist tries to become a quasi-member of the group and performs various social roles that are open to him or her, attempting in the process to understand what is going on. In the hands of a skilled practitioner, this method makes for the possibility of profound insight, but it is admittedly not very rigorous. The few attempts at replication have yielded mixed results; in fact, second studies of a given culture have often produced quite different conclusions from the first, partly no doubt because of the lapse of time between studies, but also partly because of the different interests and ideologies of the anthropologists or even because different investigators asked different questions of different informants. A conspicuous case in point is that of Margaret Mead, who in her first fieldwork in the twenties interviewed a number of teenaged girls in Samoa about their sex lives (she had been so instructed by her mentor, Franz Boas) and reported that they experienced almost total freedom in this area (Mead 1928). Years later, Derek Freeman, on the basis of investigating more "official" sources such as newspapers and adults, concluded that a naive Mead had been duped by her informants, who were merely exercising their lurid imaginations (Freeman 1983). He may well have been right; but it is also quite possible that Mead was also right, but that what the young people did was outside the attention of adults.

Anthropologists—and for that matter sociologists—in the functional mode did tend to exaggerate greatly the degree of uniformity and unanimity in the cultures they studied. The common practice in field anthropology of using as informants a few persons of prestige and power, coupled with functional theory, often led anthropologists to create an artificially edenic and harmonious picture of the community under study. The "anthropology and sociology of what is" tended to credit information from "official" sources, such as elderly males, rather than from dissident sources. Powerful voices were affirmed, weak voices were silenced. Female field investigators, and more recently post-modernism, have undermined this happy exercise in false consensus and highlighted oppression and conflict. But then, Marx had already done that more than a century earlier.

Because anthropologists work constantly in the uncertainties and discrepancies of alien worldviews, they have for long been more aware than most other social scientists that both epistemology and ethics are to a greater or lesser degree cultural artifacts. This is in fact precisely why they devised the concept of *cultural relativity*, already mentioned above, which asserts that what is seen as real and true, what is seen as good or bad, are not universally the same but differ depending on what culture one is considering. And because the criteria by which judgments are made are themselves culturally variable, it is inappropriate to apply standards from one culture in evaluating the phenomena of another culture. This concept was devised by people like Boas and Malinowski (see above) quite explicitly to combat the rampant racism and ethnocentrism that had previously been endemic not only in Western societies at large but also in evolutionary models of the social sciences.

The difficulty, of course, lies in knowing how far to go in this direction. Could one say, for example, that a view of the nature of reality that is normal for a Buddhist would be delusional for a modern Westerner? Or could one say that infanticide as practiced in ancient Rome, the self-immolation of widows formerly practiced in India, or wife lending as practiced by the Inuit, were acceptable because they were approved by the rules of their respective societies? Even the most radical relativists among anthropologists refuse categorically to accept Hitler's "final solution," the extermination of the Jews, as a mere quirk of German culture; but on what basis can they make such a judgment? Hatch (1983) has an excellent treatment of the dilemmas posed by cultural relativity for its proponents. Most disconcerting to many classical anthropologists has been the recent move, stimulated by postmodernism, to turn the critique of cultural relativity upon anthropology itself, and to accuse the very discipline that invented the concept of being conceptually imperialistic! The accusation stems from the fact that anthropologists willy-nilly make use of heuristic and putatively universal categories in analyzing cultures: such categories as marriage, art, religion, have been questioned as supposedly Western rather than universal. We will deal with the thorny issues involved, as well as the relations of this concept to the sociology of knowledge and to postmodernism, in Chapter 5.

Anthropological linguistics must be mentioned, partly because it has been important in supporting strongly the concept of "rules" and "rule-like behavior" in the social sciences. From its close study of the nature of language, it has emphasized the conventional, even arbitrary connection between form and meaning, basic to the field since the work of Ferdinand de Saussure in the first two decades of this century. But the emphasis on rigor in the statement and application of the rules of phonology and grammar has led some linguists to a neglect of the intrinsic nexus between language and culture that alone gives language the meanings it is intended to express but is more complex and messier, and therefore harder to reduce to rules. It is at this point, however, that Christian missionary agencies, notably the Summer Institute of Languages (SIL), as well as scholars of the United Bible Societies (UBS), have made a sterling contribution. No one has tackled, analyzed, and described more exotic languages than have missionaries. This has usually been done with the ultimate purpose of making the Bible available in these languages. But in the process they have provided the discipline with an enormous mountain of primary data. And some few of them, notably Kenneth L. Pike of SIL and Eugene A. Nida of UBS, have made notable contributions to linguistic theory.

Psychology

Psychology is probably the least "social" of the social sciences, because of its long-term tendency to focus largely on the individual person as a quasi-monad. This focus is, of course, an expression of the individualism gone-to-seed that characterizes Western societies.

In psychology, the earliest important work was done out of a medical background by people such as Wundt (e.g., *Grundzuger der physiologischen Psychologie*, 1873–74), William James (e.g., *The Varieties of Religious Experience*, 1902), and Freud (e.g. *The Interpretation of Dreams*, 1900, and *The Origin and Development of Psycho-Analysis*, 1910). Because of its origins in medicine, psychology is the one social science that remains unabashedly committed to therapy; that is, to a real-world use for its insights.

Psychology has developed a number of different theories of personality, a number of theories to account for mental and emotional disorders (the prevalent model being that of "illness"), and a number of therapies to deal with these disorders. But psychology and its medical extension, psychiatry, have never developed any single convincing model that has dominated the field, whether in diagnosis, in prognosis, or in therapy. Currently, the great unresolved divide in the therapeutic field is between those psychologists and psychiatrists who see disorders as caused primarily by physical factors, and therefore amenable to chemical (or electrical) therapy, and those who insist on psychogenic causes, and therefore use psychotherapy (ridiculed by others as "mere talking").

Psychology's most extreme attempt to be rigorously empirical is behaviorism, the reduction of human behavior to a stimulus-response and operant conditioning model attributable ultimately to Pavlov and his dogs, but applied to human beings by people like Thorndike and Skinner (Skinner 1971). The focus on behavior to the exclusion of internal mental states and processes reflects the determination to be "scientific," that is, empirical. Because no one has access to what goes on inside the "black box" that is the mind, it cannot be studied "scientifically." Skinner argued that human beings and their behaviors are totally conditioned, even determined, by the conditions in which they live. Freedom and dignity are, therefore, illusions. He further insisted that to a scientist like himself, to understand the roots of human behavior is to be able to control it and he devised a system of what he called "operant conditioning" to implement this view. "Behavior modification" in this mode has enjoyed some use in treating behavior problems in children and convicts. But it seems to me that this model falls far short of explaining even human *behavior* in its totality, let alone personality, emotions, moods, and the perturbations of these mental experiences; it leads, in my judgment, to rigorous triviality. As a matter of fact, behaviorism as a theory seems to have lost most of its influence in psychology.

At the opposite extreme stands psychoanalysis in the Freudian mold, with its enormous reliance on the intuitions of the analyst and its unapologetic use of mythic concepts like id, ego, libido, and Oedipus complex. Ironically, although psychoanalysis is in serious decline among scholars and therapists, it continues to enjoy, usually in greatly distorted form, popularity in the educated and semieducated public.

One fairly well-defined field within psychology is due to the genius of the Swiss scholar Piaget—the field he called developmental psychology. Its concern is with the mental, emotional, and moral development of children through specific stages. Piaget was concerned to demonstrate that children think and respond differently from adults, and that the differences are due to the regular process of maturation from birth to adulthood. Various Christian thinkers, especially in the field of religious education, have borrowed from Piaget and his disciplines. One strong criticism I have is that developmental psychology offers no account of the less worthy of the impulses of children: whence does naughtiness come? No psychology that fails to take sin into consideration will do the job. (Nor, of course, can any other social science.)

Social psychology has in recent decades somewhat tempered this narrowness of concern by seeing the individual's personality development and pathologies in the matrix of family and social group. This field is also, unlike the rest of psychology, one of the most developed areas in social science, with well-established theories supported by well-conceived and well-replicated laboratory research. Social psychology has, along with its theoretical elaboration, been found quite useful therapeutically, especially in emphasizing the frequent sociogenetic components in psychological disorders, as in the concept of co-dependence in addicts.

Most psychologists and psychiatrists work in fact with a rather eclectic mix of models that deal with personality, self, persona, and the disorders of persons. It also seems to be the case that psychology, especially in its more popular expressions, is particularly vulnerable to specious or at least poorly founded fads. In fact, the jargon generated by these fads has aptly been called "psychobabble." There is a great deal of talk, for instance, about persons being "poorly adjusted" or "well-adjusted," the latter meaning that the person in question is able to function socially and professionally with a minimum of disturbances and conflicts; in other words, that the person has internalized the beliefs, values, and attitudes of society, that he or she has made them an integral part of the personality. The question is, of course, whether society itself has an accurate understanding of reality such that it merits one's "adjusting" to it. In other words, if society's views are substantively incorrect, if society is to some significant degree mad, would not sanity call for the persons to be *mal*adjusted (see Rom. 12:2)?

Economics

Economics abstracts, from the tangled complex of human relationships and behaviors, those that have to do with the production, distribution, and use of goods and services. Thus, it has traditionally studied markets and other forms of exchange, production and distribution, labor and management, and increasingly in the last few decades, money and the transfer and exchange of currency. In this section, I am deeply indebted to Robert Heilbroner's *The Worldly Philosophers* (1953), which remains, despite its age, a classic exposition of the story of economics.

Economists often aspire to, and claim, great precision in their use of statistical and econometric analysis. But to an outside observer, the different results achieved by different scholars and the conflicting answers they assert to the questions they investigate reflect how much they are controlled by the ideologies that they bring to their studies in the first place.

To begin with, economics became possible as a discipline only when the market achieved autonomy from other forms of social organization and control. Heilbroner argues that all societies need to coordinate economic activities in order to determine what is produced, by what means ("how"), and for whom. Historically, three systems have been created by humans to solve the tension between the selfish and anarchic impulses of persons and the need for social coordination and control: cultural and/or religious tradition, centralized authority, or the market. The possible coexistence of these systems seems not to have occurred as an answer to many. It was only in the eighteenth century that the market gained its freedom from the control of cultural and ecclesiastical tradition and centralized governmental authority and permitted profit to be an independent and powerful motivation for action. This is not to suggest that greed and selfishness were novelties, but only that allowing the profit motive to be free from other controls was a novelty. It was this novelty that opened the way for economics to emerge; the new system demanded a legitimating and explanatory philosophy.

This philosophy was provided by Adam Smith in *The Wealth of Nations* (1776). It was his self-appointed task to discover the "laws" of the market. Smith argued, in the context of what remained a basically handcraft style of production, for the greatest possible freedom for the market to regulate itself without interference from government. He felt sure that if everyone were free in the marketplace to pursue his or her own self interests, the "invisible hand" of the market would overrule and bring about the common good. This invisible hand stood in conscious contrast to the very visible hand of the government that dominated the mercantilist system that existed in the eighteenth century. The hand of the government was to be replaced by the acts of many buyers and sellers voluntarily interacting in the market. In the system Smith knew, a manufacturing establishment was just that—an enterprise where things were made by hand. The enterprise consisted of a master—the proprietor—a few journeymen who could legitimately aspire to become masters, and a few apprentices who could legitimately aspire to become journeymen. The gap between master and apprentice was not uncrossable, and human relationships between them often mitigated any harshness the system might suggest. Cooperation within a single shop was taken for granted, and competition between shops was assumed to be benign. Given these circumstances, Smith might be forgiven for taking a somewhat idyllic view of the free market. Because he was "the economist of preindustrial capitalism, he did not see the market threatened by enormous enterprises or his laws of accumulation and population upset by sociological developments fifty years off" (Heilbroner 1953:67).

The "how" question mentioned above required decisions about the coordination of the resources needed for production: land and its products, labor, and capital. Before market capitalism, "Work was not yet a means to an end [i.e., profit], work was an end in itself" (Heilbroner 1953:16). (Making work a means to an end other than itself was one dimension of what Marx later called "alienation.") In fact, capitalism converted all three of the major resources/means of any economic system into commodities; but it was not without a struggle: "To make capitalists out of guild masters meant that the laws of the jungle had to be taught to the timid denizens of the barnyard" (20), and they were quite reluctant at first. But they did learn, as Stackhouse makes clear: "The 'new science' of economics 'proved' that humanity was really a calculating creature, and that the social order found cohesion in the providential 'hidden hand' of the free market, where each made a private decision" (Stackhouse 1984:115); but collectively the system was supposed to create the greatest happiness at the most beneficial cost.

Gradually, a new form of enterprise emerged—the joint-ownership (stock) company. This was in response to the need to enlarge available resources to cover increasing start-up costs of production. This, by the way, is increasingly the case today, when the requirements of large-scale high-tech manufacturing almost preclude private funding. It was also a response to the diminishing government involvement in the planning and control of production. During the early exploration of America, for instance, as trading companies lost the support of "the crown," they offered shares of ownership to the public. But the impersonality of the corporation could and did lead to abuses, a point unmentioned by Heilbroner. When entrepreneurs discovered that economic considerations pressed them toward decisions and actions they found repugnant or overly risky if undertaken by them as individuals, they also discovered that the corporation that they had created for quite other reasons, "with all the rights and privileges of *persona ficta*, but free of the moral constraints because it had no 'soul'" (Stackhouse 1984:114), also served nicely to justify these otherwise unjustifiable decisions and actions.

Incidentally, because Heilbroner makes the case that the market system was a novelty at this time, it seems possible that the "laws" Smith and his successors followed— supply and demand, for instance—are not truly universal, but apply only in those situations where the market is the basic, taken-for-granted system of exchange. Contemporary conditions make it difficult to test this hypothesis, however, because the Western market mechanisms so thoroughly and ruthlessly dominate the global markets that alternative models would stand no chance of a valid trial.

Other factors—the rise of nation states, the wealth gained in the age of exploration, the decline of the religious spirit, urbanization, technological development, the rise of scientific curiosity—also, according to Heilbroner, contributed greatly to the emergence of market capitalism.

As the factory system sprang up, all kinds of perturbations troubled the economy of England, especially taking the form of bitter competition between the landlords, who dominated agriculture via the corn laws, and the owners of the novel factories. In this context, Ricardo developed his theory of the distribution of wealth. He argued that under prevalent law, wages were kept at subsistence level, profits of factories were nil, and all gains went to the landlords. The only equitable solution, for him, was the repeal of the corn laws and a free market.

John Stuart Mill, in *Principles of Political Economy* (1848), was much more optimistic. His major point was that "the true province of economic law was production and not distribution" (126). This was because production dealt with real, natural things—soil, resources, labor—and was therefore subject to the natural laws that governed these things. But once things were produced, distribution was the domain of free choice and economic organizations and institutions.

Decades after Smith, Marx was facing the depredations in human terms of the early industrial system, in which the invisible hand was not accomplishing much by way of defending the interests of helpless laborers faced with all-powerful factory owners. In *The Communist Manifesto* (1848), he called for a revolution by workers against the intolerable conditions of their work. In *Das Kapital* (1860s–1880s), he argued that the industrial system *alienated* workers from their work and its products, for these belonged to the factory owners rather than to those who had toiled to make them; from their fellow-laborers, for workers were in competition for too few jobs; and even from themselves, for they did not understand the nature of their problem and what they might do to rectify it. Marx in fact posited a permanent state of *conflict* between *classes*: those on the one hand who de facto owned "the means of production"—for example, land in an agricultural economy, factories in an industrial economy—and those on the other hand who owned only their labor power. What made the system doomed to self-destruction was that, as Marx saw it, those who owned the means of production also controlled both government and church to their advantage. Thus, as economic crises occurred, capital would accumulate in the hands of fewer and fewer people, and workers would be subjected to increasing misery, unemployment, and degradation. These conditions would eventually create the conditions for *revolution*, repeated as many times as necessary until a classless society—a truly *communistic* society—was inaugurated. But Heilbroner is careful to point out that, however hot his moral indignation against oppressive conditions, Marx was in his analysis coldly objective: he was determined to discover the true state of affairs and only then to vent his outrage at it.

Other nineteenth-century thinkers, a few of them motivated by Christian commitment, argued instead for reform via government action, either in regulating the conditions of labor—such as laws about the labor of women and children, laws permitting unions, laws specifying minimum wages—or in regulating the relations between industry and the customer, or—more recently—between industry and the environment. According to some thinkers, central banks ought also to take a more active role in regulating the money supply so as to minimize the cycles of boom and bust that characterized the nineteenth and twentieth centuries. Others think this approach is obsolete. From fairly early times, Europe and the United States followed different paths in this regard. For various reasons that lie outside our concern here, European countries developed a quite strong and elaborate network of assistance for the unfortunate (and correspondingly higher taxes), which had no counterpart in the United States until after the Great Depression. Then a generation of economists, including the Englishman Keynes and the American Galbraith, argued for the kind of government activism that characterized Roosevelt's New Deal in the 1930s, the policies of Labor governments in the United Kingdom, and Johnson's Great Society in the 1960s. More recently, a generation of "neoclassical" economists arose that shaped the thinking of the Reagan administration in the United States and the Thatcher administration in the United Kingdom. But it is interesting to note that neoclassical economists in Europe still accept and even welcome a degree of intervention and regulation by government that is anathema to American economists of this school.

A minority of economists maintain a link with ethics—what Adam Smith called "moral philosophy"—that the discipline as a whole, in its reductionistic focus on the market and its posture of so-called objectivity, has forsaken. Thus, Kenneth Boulding could write a book under the title *The Economy of Love and Fear* (1973), in which he pointed out the important, unavoidable, and indispensable role played by charity, on the one hand, and the mechanisms of taxes, fines, and damages on the other. Earlier, Boulding had argued (1969) that economics *must* be a moral science, because every choice between alternative propositions that involves more than one person is a moral choice; and that "as science develops, it no longer merely investigates the world; it creates the world which it is investigating." Therefore it must take seriously the moral dimensions of what it is doing, for it has real consequences. E. F. Schumacher wrote *Small Is Beautiful: Economics as if People Mattered* (1973) as a counter to the abuses that often accompany "economies of scale," especially in relations between the First World and the Third. More recently, Jane Collier has described and deplored in a number of stimulating works (1992) what she has called "economism"—the dominance over all domains of Western life of a narrow economic ideology divorced from ethical concerns and detrimental to genuine human concerns. Also, under the auspices of the World Council of Churches, Bob Goudzwaard and Harry de Lange have written *Beyond Poverty and Affluence: Toward an Economy of Care* (1986) to propose a less predatory model of economic relations. Heilbroner, in a short article (1995), points out that economists are not mere disinterested observers, for their policy recommendations involve choices that benefit some people and disadvantage others. When, for example, the Federal Reserve Board raises interest rates to stop inflation, it also increases unemployment (and when unemployment rises, so does the stock market, because this means that labor costs will be held down!). "What is . . . being held at bay are our moral values. For there is another, less unfair, means of controlling inflation: raising federal taxes" (Heilbroner 1995:20). But

the discipline as a whole tends, as Heilbroner says, to ethical indifference, in the misplaced confidence that the
economy operates according to scientific "laws" that ought
not—indeed, that cannot—be tampered with. In such a
context, it must be pointed out that a marketplace totally
unregulated is nothing more nor less than the economic
version of Darwinism.

Given this fact, it is not a little ironic that the Darwinian
free-market ideology has found some of its most ardent
advocates among Christians who are bitterly opposed to
biological Darwinism. They enthusiastically defend it on
the basis of biblical texts and snippets, often taken out of
context; and they insist on interpreting literally any passage that seems to support their position, and to insist that
passages that do not support it, such as the Sermon on the
Mount (Matt 5–7) and the story of the rich young man (Mark
10:17–22), must be taken as figurative or as hyperbole.

The colonial system greatly altered the terms of the
market for industrialized countries. As the search in the
non-Western world for sources of cheap resources and
cheap labor led to wholesale conquest and exploitation of
these erstwhile remote parts of the world, "The colonies
were now the proletariat's proletariat" (Heilbroner
1953:198). Workers in the industrialized countries began
to prosper at the expense of the peoples of what later
became the Third World. It remained for Lenin later to
develop a full-fledged theory of imperialism, in which the
world was divided between the center (rich and powerful)
and the periphery (poor, powerless, and exploited).

Whether or not economics has any moral accountability has become an even more urgent issue in the last few
decades, as the prior colonial, mercantilist system (each
colonial power maintaining a monopoly on commerce with
its own colonies) has given way to a global market economy
that is far more ruthlessly imperial than any preceding system, whether economic, political, or religious. Economic

globalization is the predominant international reality, and all countries are being forced into the global economy willy-nilly, under irresistible pressure from the developed powers and their economic instruments, the World Bank and the International Monetary Fund. Both former colonies and former communistic societies are being subjected to "recommendations" that apparently make sense to the lenders of money but play havoc with the lives of the poorest and most powerless people. And the increasing hegemony of the economic sector over all other areas of life—politics, arts, and entertainment, even religion—needs to be understood and critiqued from a Christian ethical perspective.

Almost all of what I have been saying so far deals with macroeconomics—the economics of nations and of the global market. But microeconomics—the economic values, attitudes, and behaviors of persons—is also important in its own right. Here economics has developed the model of the *Homo economicus*, the economic actor who is ruled entirely by rational assessment of all available information and makes economic decisions uninfluenced by emotions and especially unaffected by the person's social relationships. This radically asocial notion of the individual economic actor is the target of a devastating critique by a pair of anthropologists (Douglas and Ney 1998), who point out that people in fact make decisions on the basis of all kinds of nonrational factors, and definitely in the midst of a dynamic social context of relations. Limited as it is, however, this is one model in the social sciences in which persons exercise freedom and in which their choices enter decisively into the chains of cause-and-effect.

Political Science

Political science studies the allocation, legitimation, and exercise of power in social groups—power to define and implement the aims of the group. Thus, it addresses itself to the structures and processes by which group or societal decisions are made and carried out: who is chosen to lead and how, how leadership is exercised, and so on. This means, of course, that a central topic of study is government, the practical arrangement by which societal decisions are made and implemented. For the most part, political scientists have studied Western forms of government, leaving the study of more exotic, non-Western, and especially "primitive" forms to anthropologists. In studying government, political scientists analyze both the formal structures (constitutions, legal codes) and the actual processes (political parties, elections, lobbying, etc.). The realm of international relations and international law, international organizations, and multinational blocs, as well as war and peace, also falls into the scope of political science.

Political science arose, as Milbank has shown (1990), out of the efforts of political philosophers from Plato and Aristotle to Machiavelli, Hobbes, Locke, and company. It began to aspire, at least in the minds of some of its practitioners, to scientific status early in the present century. The shift is described by Minogue as follows:

> The scientific study of politics is, then, a great but limited achievement of our century. Like any other form of understanding, it gains its power from its limitations, but it happens that the specific limitations of science in its fullest sense are especially restrictive in the understanding of human life (1995:98).

But the shift was initially accepted by only some political scientists, so that for a time there was little consensus and considerable disarray in the discipline. Both Easton (1968) and Somit and Tanenhaus (1982) presented political science as riddled with controversy over basic issues. First, what is the unit of study? Second, what methods should be used? As to the unit of study, some argued that it should be institutional entities, such as the state; others insisted that it should be actual political behaviors, that is, the way politics is played out in action. As for method, there remained some who insisted on what they call a "classical" approach (Bull 1966), in which political science was closely related to history; others, such as Kaplan (1969), agreed with Minogue that political science should be scientific in the same sense as the natural sciences; various scholars called for the formulation of "laws" on the example of economics. The classicists argued that by insisting on a scientific method, the scientists precluded any depth of understanding. The classicists thus ranged themselves on the side of the interpretive school of thought in the social sciences. The scientists argued, of course, that the classical approach was muddled and unrigorous, mixing facts and value judgments in a sloppy way.

Today, however, though there is still no more philosophical unanimity than in the other social sciences, and all kinds of positions from neopositivism to postmodernism find their advocates, political science is much more orderly. There are a number of clear subdisciplines, each of which is internally relatively coherent, and there is a good bit of cross-fertilization between them.

A very basic question addressed by political science is, Why any government? The answer, clearly, is that human beings and groups are not naturally self-regulating. Most people experience both social and antisocial impulses; they need to have the positive impulses encouraged and the negative ones discouraged. And the group, whether a nomadic band of thirty pastoralists dominated by a patriarch or a modern nation state of one billion people governed by a parliamentary system, needs to have its interests defined and its directions spelled out in some orderly and fully acknowledged manner. Otherwise, chaos would reign and the survival of all would be jeopardized. But in order to serve its functions, government needs both power—the ability to implement its decisions—and authority or legitimacy—the public recognition of its right to govern. Power without legitimacy, which is tyranny, will ultimately be rejected; legitimacy without power is ineffectual. In other words, governments need the ability to enforce their authority. Many political scientists argue, therefore, that a centrally defining property of government is the monopoly on the legitimate use of force or lethal violence, whether in internal affairs (e.g., keeping the peace) or in external relations (waging war). Generally speaking, then, governments exist to minimize conflict and to maximize cooperation.

But even more important than the security that governmental power offers is the question of how that power is exercised. St. Augustine correctly argued in *The City of God* that justice is "the foundation of the state." Justice in the biblical sense, it seems to me, involves at least three components: at the simplest level, punishment of lawbreakers and protection and vindication for the law abiding (Rom 13); second, in the judicial system, to eliminate as far as possible the influence of any factor—such as the wealth or poverty of defendants and litigants—that is irrelevant to the case, so that each is judged on its merits alone (numerous passages in the Mosaic Law, Proverbs, and the prophets); and finally, in the economic realm, assuring that children are neither privileged unduly for the merits of their parents nor penalized unduly for the delinquencies of their parents; put otherwise, to ensure that privilege or penalty do not become cumulative through the generations (Lev 25). This last, if it had ever been practiced in ancient Israel, would have been an important mechanism fostering the larger concern of distributive justice—the effort to make sure that everyone gets what is equitably due to him or her, neither more nor less. A government that does not rule justly loses its legitimacy before God. But there are limits to what any government can do by the means at its disposal: legislation, regulation, and coercive enforcement.

The question of justice in all three senses is much discussed in political science. The political doctrine of democracy, for instance, includes a lively concern for equality of opportunity, and sometimes even of outcomes. Many studies of revolutions or civil dissent, for instance, focus on injustice as a major factor in these upheavals.

The Social Sciences as "Sciences"

All of these disciplines have had, as I have suggested, a very hard time becoming "scientific" in the sense in which that term applies to the physical sciences. Kuhn (1970) took pleasure in pointing out that although the physical sciences worked on the basis of elaborate and sophisticated "paradigms," the social sciences were in fact "preparadigmatic"; that is, they had developed nothing that could be dignified with the term *theory*. In trying to resolve this problem, these disciplines have too often taken one or the other of two paths. Either, like behaviorism in psychology, they have decided to be scientific at all costs by limiting themselves to empirical data, in which case they have lapsed into triviality. Or they have tried various uneasy compromises between what is considered rigor in science on the one hand, and serious understanding on the other. But because of persistent feelings of insecurity vis-à-vis the natural scientists, some social scientists are much addicted to what Laver has called "the obfuscation of the obvious" (1983:13), by which he means the use of ponderous, turgid jargon and style to express banalities and platitudes in the effort to sound impressive and learned.

One major effort to establish and enhance the scientific status of these disciplines was the multivolume *International Encyclopedia of the Social Sciences* (1968). It is an exceedingly valuable collection, but it in the end merely documents a specific moment in the history of the field.

The passage from "philosophy" to "science" as regards the human phenomenon entailed two subsidiary passages:

(1) from the normative to the descriptive; as Laver puts it: social scientists are "more concerned with how things *are* than with how they *should be*" (1983:5); and (2) from the rational to the empirical. Thus, "natural law" in the social sciences was a halfway house between the law of God and the laws of nature. Natural law retained a strong component of normativity while eliminating its grounding in God. But without God, normativity is vacuous, arbitrary, and easily totalitarian; which is why cultural relativity and postmodernism have had such a field day attacking it.

One of the most important contrasts between the physical or natural sciences and the social sciences is the ability of the former to conduct a wide variety of controlled experiments with a minimum of either practical or ethical objection. The social sciences, on the other hand, are extremely limited in how and how much they may experiment with their subjects. Strong ethical concerns are quite properly expressed when certain experiments are proposed. In some cases, scientists have jeopardized the freedom and dignity of their subjects. In the case of experiments conducted by Hitler's scientists on Jewish and other despised subjects, life itself was expendable, and anything became permissible. Sadly, humiliating, dangerous, and even fatal experiments on human beings, especially unfree human beings, are not unknown in other Western countries.

Another significant difference between the social sciences and the physical sciences, as I pointed out in an earlier chapter, is that the social sciences are reflexive; that is, researchers are themselves part of the human scene that they are investigating and cannot entirely escape the subjective biases that this fact creates.

It is for this reason, among others, that a more effective third strategy ought to be followed—to redefine the social sciences as interpretive or hermeneutical sciences rather than as explanatory sciences. This, it would seem, ought to be satisfactory. But, as Hekman says, a positivist stance is far from dead, if only to resist the nihilism of postmodernism:

> The positivist research program in the social sciences that has been seriously discredited in recent decades still serves as the basis for most social scientific research. It has not been replaced by any of the alternative programs that have been proposed, first, because no unanimity exists as to which of these alternatives should be adopted and, secondly, because none of these alternatives offers what appears to social scientists to be a viable method for social scientific research. As a result, as many have argued, the social sciences are cast adrift without a theoretical anchor (Hekman 1986:1).

To summarize: the perennial pressure within the social sciences to be scientific on the example of the natural sciences in the face of the evident impossibility of studying the human phenomenon with the methods of the natural sciences has led to three distinct responses: (1) to cut the subject to fit the method, as in behaviorism (i.e., reductionism); (2) to admit that these disciplines were not science at all, but something else, such as history (this was a decidedly minority position); or (3) to stretch the methods and definition of science to include hermeneutical disciplines. In addition to reductionism, which I will discuss further later, the pressure to be scientific also sometimes led to the reluctance to apply one's science to the real world in a committed manner, as we saw in Chapter 1. These features of the social sciences also led to a number of other damaging tendencies, which I will discuss in Chapter 5.

The Social Sciences as "Useful"

What I wrote in Chapter 1 about the shift in the social sciences from utopianism to a "scientific" perspective should

not be understood to mean that committed, intervention-
ist social science simply disappeared; it merely went on its
way as a minority project, which merits some consideration in its own right. Utility did take a back seat for many,
as an anecdote illustrates. Early in my graduate studies in
anthropology, I asked my major professor what was the use
of anthropology. He replied, "It's no use at all, it's fun!" But
remnants of the old idealism remained in the corners of the
social sciences, as a few examples will show.

Not a few people with social science training participated in the "Brain Trust" that advised Franklin Delano
Roosevelt in designing his New Deal in the 1930s. The
Swedish scholar Gunnar Myrdal wrote *An American
Dilemma* (1944) to address the race problem in the United
States (it was Myrdal, by the way, who coined the phrase
"social engineering"). Today, quite a few economists and
political scientists participate full- or part-time in various
government policy-planning ventures (Douglas and Ney
1998), and quite a few others hope that their research will
be of use in the real world. But these authors, although
applauding the intention to utility, deplore what they see as
a truncated view of the human person that prevails in policy-planning circles: in this narrow view, which has been
called the *Homo economicus* view, the human person is
someone who rationally pursues his or her economic interests in total isolation from cultural factors and especially in
isolation from the social context. It is the ultimate in individualism. Incidentally, economics as a whole tends to be
strongly committed to be useful to the market, that is, to
private business and its auxiliary agencies.

Then there are "applied anthropology" and "action
anthropology." The first began when various anthropologists, professional and amateur, in the British colonial
empire and in the Bureau of Indian Affairs in the United
States among others, devised and engaged in "applied
anthropology" to ensure that the policies of the governing

powers should without fail be implemented, but with as little trauma as possible for the subject peoples. In this mode, anthropologists used their insights into the local cultures as a base from which to explain and justify colonial policies and so to induce the people to conform to these policies voluntarily. In other words, the clout of anthropological sophistication was added to the coercive power of the colonial governments to undermine the self-defined interests and aspirations of the people. Sol Tax, by way of intentional contrast to applied anthropology, devised "action anthropology" in order to place the powers and resources of the anthropologist at the disposition of the subject peoples in their unequal struggles against the dominant powers (Tax 1975; Stanley 1975). For instance, in a situation of conflict between Native Americans on a reservation and local school authorities who wanted the Indian children to go to local schools, Tax placed his knowledge of American law at the disposal of the Indians. He explained the intentions of the local Anglo authorities, but he also helped the Indians formulate their own options so that they could struggle for their own interests on a more even playing field.

Anthropologists also participated in the war effort during World War II by creating cultural studies of "the enemy" (e.g., Benedict 1946). Later, during the Vietnam War, anthropologists were employed by the U.S. military to help devise counterinsurgency programs in Southeast Asia, and information generated by anthropologists was used to do actual harm to indigenous peoples. This caused a scandal in the American Anthropological Association and occasioned much soul-searching in the discipline, endless correspondence in the professional newsletters, and a long-drawn-out effort to formulate professional ethics for anthropologists. For a balanced discussion of the whole issue of anthropological intervention in social reality, in particular under colonialism, see Keesing (1976:526–45).

Similarly, psychology was mobilized to produce war propaganda during World War II and since. And, of course, there is the major commitment of psychology to a therapeutic model and to usefulness in the healing of psychic disorders.

Not all of these efforts represent idealism, though most reflect some measure of ideological commitment, whether to the left or to the right, to free-market capitalism or to socialism, and often simply to democracy, or, more broadly, to social justice. Marxism also has exercised some influence in the social sciences, so that commitment to a cause was in those quarters considered not only legitimate, but mandatory. But all these efforts to make the social sciences useful in the real world, whatever the interests they served, have in the present century usually been considered marginal and less than scientific by the dominant ethos of the disciplines, for they were in one way or another ideologically committed and therefore not "objective." Quite a few social scientists have wisely chosen, like Marx, to be rigorously objective in their research to discover what is the state of affairs and then to find ways of making an impact on the world with their findings.

The Social Sciences—Separate or Together

Though these disciplines display a great deal of overlapping in their areas of concern, and major concepts continually flow from one to the others, each of these disciplines has tended, especially in the recent past, to insist on its own autonomy and to work in its own field with a minimum of contact with the others. This isolation is, however, decreasing, and, happily, a growing number of interdisciplinary projects are being undertaken. But each discipline has tended to look at human beings and human groups and social arrangements and processes from its own single narrow perspective and to ignore the rest of reality as irrelevant to its concerns. Thus, for instance, Durkheim was passionately committed to creating a sociology that owed nothing to the characteristics of the individual members of the societies it studied and was therefore totally independent of psychology. But in neglecting the complex and inextricable interconnections between persons, groups, institutions, and the ideas that they share and that make them all workable, these sciences achieve only a very modest and often superficial degree of understanding. Reductionism is a powerful urge in the social sciences, but it produces fragmented insight.

The autonomy claimed by each of these disciplines, especially economics and political science, surely reflects the autonomy claimed by the institutions they study. During the entire modern era, both the state and the market have increasingly insisted on their sovereignty within their own domains, free from the rule of other institutions, especially the church. Machiavelli on the one hand, and Adam Smith on the other, articulated the grounds for these demands. But Caesar has always aspired to be god, and the modern nation state is no exception. Today, in the United States, it is the structures of the state, especially the law courts, that exercise the power, without appeal, to define the boundaries between church and state and to regulate what may and what may not be done in the name of religion; the pity is that, by and large, the church supinely allows this to go on without a protest. As for the market, it is increasingly dominant over every other institution in society, including the church, which is being reinterpreted and redefined in economic terms, as we will show in Chapter 5.

There have been significant interactions between these disciplines, and the number is growing. In fact, in the United States the National Science Foundation favors interdisciplinary research projects.

One notable example of interdisciplinary work involves anthropology and psychology. Several anthropologists have made use of psychology and its tools (e.g., Thematic

Apperception Tests) in their fieldwork and in studies of child-rearing practices and their consequences. They have also used psychological tools and concepts in a number of studies of "national character/personality." Anthropologists and psychologists and psychiatrists have collaborated in studying the cultural patterning of mental illness, its symptoms and description, and appropriate therapies. But for the most part, these cooperative ventures have remained marginal to the disciplines involved.

It should also be pointed out that in recent years sociology and anthropology have experienced a partial convergence in methods, as more and more anthropologists have studied aspects of Western cultures and some sociologists have studied non-Western societies. Both use comparative methods, which used to be a monopoly of anthropology; and both use statistical methods, which used to be a monopoly of sociology.

The Social Sciences and the Human

The social sciences' picture of what it means to be human finds itself in many ways radically in contrast with the picture given in the Bible, whether in its Israelite roots or in its Christian fruits. The sciences stress our kinship with the animal world; the Bible speaks of a unique "image of God" that sets us apart from our animal relatives. Humans are presented, for instance, as autonomous individuals whose relationships with others and even with God are totally optional; the Bible presents us as innately related to one another and to God. The language of the social sciences is the language of "rights" to which we are entitled, rights that we may use as we choose without restraints; the Bible presents us as recipients of God's free and generous grace, which we may accept thankfully and responsibly. The social sciences describe our emotional problems as illnesses that happen to us (passive participation) and need to be treated and cured; the Bible talks about sin that needs to be forgiven (active participation). And the social sciences, ironically, for all their talk about freedom, present us as more or less determined by heredity, nurture, or combinations thereof; the Bible speaks of freedom given by God that we may enjoy as God's children. We will say more of these issues in Chapter 5.

Reductionism and interdisciplinary isolation have also produced, as I mentioned earlier, a *fragmented* picture of human beings, torn between disparate and often incompatible roles. Economists insist on persons as producers, sellers, buyers, and consumers of goods and services, motivated entirely by that dynamic. Employers informed by this vision insist that employees sacrifice everything else to their jobs. Political scientists see us primarily as citizens and voters, whereas sociologists describe us as acting out our appropriate roles as spouses, parents, children, and the like. The result is that we often make conscious and often awkward shifts from role to role, and compromises when roles conflict; and if we are not careful, we end up with no "self" to coordinate the various roles. The modern self, in other words, is not coherent or integrated, not centered; we seem to have as many "selves" as we have roles to play. Might it be that the phenomenon of split or multiple personality is merely an extreme, pathological form of our experience in everyday life?

The clash between roles can be seen in extreme form in the case of persons who find themselves required to do things in one role that radically contradict the actions required by other roles—for instance, the "good family men and women" who were Hitler's torturers and executioners. It is becoming increasingly common in Western countries that the "secular" roles Christians are called upon to play in society come into conflict with their Christian and/or ethical convictions. William Jennings Bryan, Secretary of State under Wilson, resigned rather than participate in Wilson's call for a declaration of war against Germany.

One matter that is especially salient in anthropology because of its focus on the exotic, and because anthropology includes a biological component, is the status of humankind as, on the one hand, a single species (which, when properly understood, underlines its unity and the high degree of homogeneity it displays); and, on the other hand, as a congeries of different societies, communities, classes, "races," and the like (which underlines its diversity and conflicts). The dominant rationalist strand in the Enlightenment stressed the unity of humankind: it propagated such notions as "universal grammar" (taken up in this century by the school of Noam Chomsky), "the universal rights of man," "the psychic unity of mankind," and the like. The contrary emphasis on particularity and locality was stressed by the romantic strand of the Enlightenment, especially in Germany. Here we find the emphasis on *das Volk*, which has had both benign and profoundly noxious effects in the real world; for example, in the systematic racism of Hitler. The universalism of the rationalistic Enlightenment was itself not always benign, as Lasch has pointed out (1991). In ruthlessly denying the rights of particularity, it became quite totalitarian in the French Revolution, later in colonialism, and even, to some extent, in the Modern Missionary Movement. Max Stackhouse (1984:44–46) makes the plausible argument that particularism and universalism in the social sciences are, respectively, modern reflexes of the medieval philosophical positions then known as nominalism and realism. The church, via Thomas Aquinas, opted for a compromise, a moderate realism. But the realist position quickly became authoritarian, hierarchical, and reactionary, whereas from the nominalist position there later developed movements for freedoms and rights, not to speak of chaos.

The Social Sciences, Religion, and the Religions

Three of these disciplines—sociology, anthropology, and psychology—study religion as a component of their field of

concern. But because they have felt it necessary to adopt
the stance of methodological agnosticism, they have been
forced to deal reductionistically with religion, seeing it as
nothing but another worldly ideology and institution.
Thus, sociology, especially in its functionalist mode, looks
at religion as one of the institutions of society, the one that
usually supplies sacred (or supernatural, depending on the
worldview involved) sanctions in support of the profane
institutions like government, market, and social structure;
or, conversely, provides (via prophets) a sacred or supernatural judgment on the other institutions. Durkheim, for
instance, saw the religion of Australian Aborigines as centered on a totem that ultimately represented the society
itself as object of worship (1961). Before him, Marx had
seen religion as the "opiate" used by the oppressed proletariat to deaden the pain of their alienation, and provided
by the oppressors as an antidote to potential revolution.
Anthropology studies religion as essentially related to
worldview and as providing ritual confirmation, reinforce-
ment, and even dramatization of basic beliefs, values, and
attitudes; and also as providing means to cope with major
existential catastrophes. Psychology, ever since William
James (1902), has tended to look for connections between
religion and mental health or its absence. There is a real
sense in which religion can and does function in these
ways in the world of persons and institutions. It also seems
to be the case that religion has historically taken different
forms in different kinds of societies. In so-called primitive
societies, for instance, reality is one, but has both sacred
and profane aspects. In more complex societies, the sacred
separates from the profane ontologically to become the
supernatural, over and against the natural, perhaps mir-
roring the hierarchical structure of society. Finally, in modern Western societies, the supernatural has gradually
eroded for many people, and the world has once again
lapsed into a kind of one-level, monadic reality. Thus, the

scientists think, religion can be "explained" (see Preus 1987). But although the social sciences can deal more or less adequately with these this-worldly dimensions of religion, what none of them can do within its self-assigned parameters is to discuss the truth or existence or validity of the transcendent, which is the ultimate referent of religion. This, in fact, has been banned from scientific discourse ever since Comte in the 1830s. We will deal with this matter in Chapter 5.

I suggest that when the transcendent dimension is bracketed, religion either becomes "useful" toward some nontranscendent end, as Durkheim argued, or it becomes otiose. One favorite tactic of some, for instance, is to claim that one can evaluate a religion's utility by assessing its position on "fundamental human rights." This is the argument, not only of some social scientists, but also of some pluralists in the field of religion. But doing this is making one or other of three assumptions: either one assumes that human rights are sui generis and independent of, and superordinate to, all religions; or one assumes that the perspective on human rights that one holds as a part of one's own religion is universally valid; or, finally, one assumes that over and above all religions there is a knowable, divinely ordained revelation on the basis of which one may assess all religions. Frankly, the first two of these assumptions seem to be dubious in the extreme, both a priori and from empirical observation; and the third, although a priori attractive to Christians, needs to be carefully qualified if one is to avoid making superficial and inappropriate judgments.

The Social Sciences and Popular Worldviews

Perhaps it would not be amiss to make clear at this point why I think it matters, in working toward a missiology of Western cultures, to give as much consideration to the social sciences as I am doing. I do not argue that the popular worldviews of contemporary Westerners are exactly like the positions I have been describing. But I do insist that (a) these positions arise from features of the worldviews common among ordinary Western people, educated or not; and (b) even more to the point, the positions expressed by social scientists, over time, strongly influence popular worldviews. I am not suggesting that people pay a lot of attention to social scientists per se; in fact, there is often a sort of bemused, condescending contempt in popular attitudes toward social scientists. And there are almost always grotesque distortions and a greater or lesser time lag between the idea as formulated by a scientist and a belief held by many people in the street. Nevertheless, the influence, if indirect, is there; it is powerful; and it is enduring. Not infrequently, an idea becomes most powerful in the popular domain at about the time the scientists are moving on to other things. For instance, Freud is still heavily followed in the popular press, albeit in bastardized form, even though few psychologists or psychiatrists follow him today. But the notions of repression (mistranslated to mean anything resembling self-discipline), complex, unconscious (more often, "subconscious"), and the like, are part of almost everyone's vocabulary. Similarly, Darwin's basic idea has been misrepresented as "descent from the apes," and it is in that erroneous form that the issue is debated pro and con by nine people out of ten. The real or perceived determinism of social scientists translates in the popular mind into a denial of responsibility for one's actions, as anyone can attest who has sat on a jury in criminal court. Stackhouse points out that popular ideas about personhood, family, sexuality, and so on, are much influenced by psychology:

> Basic attitudes toward these matters have been deeply influenced by psychological and psychiatric findings. The giants of these sciences—Freud, Jung, Piaget, and the rest—did much of their work precisely during the great transition. Their ideas have

been imported from Europe and have become a part of the ordinary vocabulary of daily conversation of the mass media (Stackhouse 1984:95).

Nor is the influence exercised at the level of ideas only. Such powerfully seductive ideas in turn shape people's behavior in the real world. They express themselves through people's hopes, fears, ambitions, aspirations; they shape people's views of what is possible, of what is probable, of what is impossible, of what is real and unreal, of what is desirable and undesirable. We cannot afford the luxury of ignorance about these matters if we want to understand what is going on in the lives of today's Westerners.

4

The Interface

The interface between missiology and the social sciences has been exploited only episodically and superficially by missiologists. In the first place, missiology has not engaged the entire range of the social sciences. It has been involved in one way or another with cultural anthropology for over a century, no doubt largely because anthropology has directed its attention to the same exotic, and often small-scale, non-literate societies that have preoccupied missiology. The same mental distortion that Raoul Narroll years ago called "the bias of the exotic" in anthropology heavily affected missiology. These same societies have also been part of the "non-Christian world" that, in the minds of many, contrasted so sharply with the Christian world that was the West. In other words, missiology's exclusive reliance on anthropology reflected a naive "Christendom" mentality. But sociology has only fairly recently been called upon by some missiologists to help them understand modern, complex, and/or urban societies, much as anthropology had earlier been enlisted to understand "primitive" cultures.

Psychology has been called upon by a few missiologists, or more often mission administrators, concerned with counseling in a cross-cultural encounter, or wanting to help missionaries and missionaries' children cope with culture shock and other psychologically troubling experiences. Mission agencies also often use psychological instruments such as the Minnesota Multiphasic Personality Inventory (MMPI) in the process of screening candidates for missionary service, but missiologists have not looked to psychology to help them do missiology. However, it is perhaps not stretching the limits of missiology excessively, especially in a work focusing on a missiology of Western culture, to mention the enormous influence of psychology, including its theories of personality, pathology, and therapy, on the field of pastoral counseling in the United States. Thomas Oden, for one (1983), has severely, and I think properly, criticized pastoral counselors for substituting psychotherapy for pastoral counseling and the cure of souls.

I have found no evidence that missiologists qua missiologists have looked at all to political science or economics to help them do missiology. Unfortunately, this neglect often reveals a dismaying degree of ignorance and naivete among missionaries and missiologists about political and economic issues. I have mentioned in an earlier chapter that I once tried to alert a group of American missionaries from Africa and Latin America to the complexities of the relationships between the United States and the countries in which they worked, and to the pitfalls these relationships might offer for mission. The response was that America's involvement in the world was always benevolent and that I ought to be more patriotic. Generally speaking, American missionaries and even missiologists, especially among conservative evangelicals, take for granted as good and beneficent the political and economic institutions of the United States, and they are even likely to consider them as in some sense universally normative. Even those who are aware of the problem of ethnocentrism and cultural negativism in the past tend to define culture narrowly enough not to include political and economic structures and processes, and thus consider non-Western patterns fair game for criticism.

But even the encounter between missiology and cultural anthropology has so far failed to explore all of the important implications of the discipline for missions. It has, roughly speaking, moved through three phases.

1. The first explicit interaction between missionaries and anthropologists occurred in the 1860s, when missionaries served as sources of field data for the earliest anthropological theorists, who were armchair scholars. This represented a significant advance over the prior situation, in which anthropologists merely used as grist for their mills whatever data they could glean haphazardly from missionary and other writings. But anthropologists such as Edward B. Tylor actively corresponded with missionaries, asking them specific questions and suggesting specific lines of inquiry. The anthropologists involved had no personal experience of the exotic, little or no respect for the persons and cultures of the "primitive" world they theorized about, and little or no sympathy with the religious aims of the missionaries whose data they were using. There is considerable evidence that the potential for both mutual benefit and conflict was recognized early, at least by a few persons (Harris 1868). But there is no evidence known to me that at this stage (1870s–1900s) the majority of missionaries were consciously making use of the concepts and theories of the European and American scholars, or recognizing that these might be potentially troubling.

2. Almost at the same time, however—Harris himself mentioned the problem—many missionaries and anthropologists did develop a sense that they might well be hostile competitors for access to the "natives." This hostility has continued to be a dominant mode of interaction right down to the present. Various scholars have explored the reasons and bases for this attitude of mutual rejection (see

Priest 1986–87; Stipe 1980; Whiteman 1985). The tension
and the occasional confrontation range over a number of
issues. Missionaries have an avowedly religious perspective
as the foundation of all their work, and base their ontology
and their ethics on God, whereas anthropologists tend to
be agnostic or atheistic, and are especially hostile to
Christianity, the religion that probably was dominant in
their home countries and from which a number of them
consciously fled when they emerged from childhood.
Missionaries aim to convert people to faith in Christ, which
inevitably alters the culture; anthropologists, especially
during the period of the dominance of functionalism,
looked for a stable, unchanging culture as their field of
study. Missionaries at their best are motivated by love and
even respect for the people they serve: anthropologists
have usually tried to mask their own feelings and attitudes
about the peoples they study under the guise of respect and
scientific objectivity, but occasionally they have betrayed,
sometimes in personal diaries and journals, that they loved
and respected, or hated and despised these people.

3. Nevertheless, and no doubt partly because of the
insistence from the first decades of this century on fieldwork as the method par excellence of anthropologists, the
one-way traffic between missionaries and anthropologists
described above was gradually replaced by a more direct
encounter between them. Many anthropologists relied
heavily on missionaries for hospitality and for access to the
peoples they studied, though they often resented this
dependence and criticized their hosts bitterly, and in some
cases made it a point not to acknowledge their indebted-
ness. A recent blatant instance is T. O. Beidelman's *Colonial
Evangelism* (1982), which self-righteously criticizes the
missionaries he met during his fieldwork, who for their part
remember that he exploited them for his own purposes. I
have already mentioned the ethnographies of missionaries
such as Codrington and Junod. The work of Wilhelm

Schmidt, SVD, in Vienna (1939) provided a strong Roman Catholic contribution not only to ethnography but to anthropological theory (Schmidt, as we saw earlier, was a diffusionist).

Furthermore, partly as the result of the efforts of the British missiologist Edwin W. Smith (1924) and others, a larger number of missionaries and missiologists became aware of anthropology as a discipline that could help them better understand the peoples among whom they worked. This process, begun early in the twentieth century, came to full flower in the fifties and sixties, when it was taken as axiomatic, especially in the United States, that preparation for missionary service should include the study of cultural (or social) anthropology, and large programs of missionary preparation were developed in both Protestant and Roman Catholic circles that included anthropology as a major component. One thinks, to mention only two examples among a number, of the School of World Mission at Fuller Theological Seminary and the mission program at the Catholic Theological Union in Chicago.

It is significant that one major area in which anthropology was called upon to assist missions was in the field of Bible translation. Two agencies and their leaders have dominated the field in this regard. One, the Summer Institute of Linguistics/Wycliffe Bible Translators (SIL), founded in the 1930s by W. Cameron Townsend, was largely shaped by the linguist Kenneth Pike. The other, the United Bible Societies (UBS), was a truly international cooperative body involving national Bible Societies in a large number of countries. As regards Bible translation, it was Eugene A. Nida who led the way, followed by a number of translations consultants. Both Pike and Nida started out in linguistics and assumed that that was the discipline that would be most useful for Bible translators, especially in translating the Bible into languages previously unwritten. But it turned out that the really important and difficult problems in translation were not purely linguistic: they stemmed from discrepancies and clashes between the worldviews represented in the biblical texts and the worldviews of the speakers of languages into which the Bible was being translated. In other words, the difficulties were cultural. So Nida and his colleagues developed a theory of translation that drew creatively upon three disciplines: linguistics, cultural anthropology, and communications theory (see Nida and Taber 1969). Numerous publications followed, including the journal *The Bible Translator*, to help translators. And to make anthropological resources better known in the wider missionary world, UBS personnel and others founded the journal *Practical Anthropology*, which appeared quarterly from 1953 to 1971. SIL is also a major publisher of all kinds of linguistic and anthropological works, data-based, theoretical, and practical alike. For an excellent treatment of translation as a dimension of missions, see Smalley's *Translation as Mission* (1991). *Practical Anthropology*, when it was discontinued as an independent journal, was reincarnated in 1972 as *Missiology* under the auspices of the American Society of Missiology. Two of its editors have been missionary anthropologists, and anthropologically-based articles have been a continuing staple.

So it is that a fairly large number of missionary anthropologists have emerged in the heritage of Codrington, Junod, Schmidt, and Leenhardt. In fact, at least in the United States, it is probably the case today that more persons known as missiologists have been educated first in anthropology than in any other discipline, even theology. (This is because doctoral programs in missiology are extremely recent, and people have traditionally entered into the field from cognate disciplines such as theology or history.) Two names surely demand individual mention: Alan R. Tippett, an Australian Methodist missionary to Fiji, who inaugurated the role of anthropology at the School of World Mission at Fuller Theological Seminary; and Louis J.

Luzbetak, SVD, who worthily filled the shoes of his master Wilhelm Schmidt in the Society of the Divine Word. His *The Church and Cultures* (1988) is a masterpiece in which anthropology, theology, and missiology are most creatively intertwined to their mutual enrichment. More recently, Charles H. Kraft (1979) at Fuller and Robert J. Schreiter (1984) have made stellar contributions.

Yet another missiological application of the social sciences is to be found in the Church Growth Theory founded by Donald A. McGavran (see McGavran 1955; 1970). McGavran felt he was being scientific by being fiercely pragmatic (he insisted, for example, that his theory offered a technical-type method to make the church grow, whatever the theology of the practitioners), by appealing explicitly to several concepts from the social sciences, and by making extensive use of statistical methods. He himself was rather naive, both theologically and scientifically (his Ph.D. was in education), but a number of his anthropologist colleagues during the years of his leadership at the School of World Mission at Fuller Theological Seminary helped correct some of his own naivete and made significant contributions of their own to the total structure of the theory. At least one component of the theory, the Homogeneous Unit Principle (HUP), has been questioned on both theological and social-scientific grounds. Theologically, the critique has been that empirical social and cultural realities have been allowed to gain an unduly determinative status with regard to the nature of the church. Scientifically, it has been pointed out that the HUP rests on an outdated functionalist view of societies and cultures as permanently closed, self-contained realities.

Sociology has been used marginally in missions since the early part of this century to serve several purposes. A sociological analysis of sorts underlay Dennis's three-volume paean to the universally beneficial effects of modern missions in the world (1897, 1899, 1906). Missionaries working in the larger, socially more complex countries of Asia sometimes appealed to sociology to help them understand the situations in which they worked. And, at least in its use of fairly basic statistical methods, Church Growth Theory rested on sociological understandings. But for the most part, sociology was relegated to the sidelines as far as missions were concerned.

Though missiologists have tended to neglect economics and political science, the ignorance and naivete they have displayed about these sciences make it imperative that in the future, especially in designing a missiology of Western culture, they should be taken with great seriousness. The problem is that ignorance is in this instance innocent but not beneficent. That is, missiologists are not ignoring these sciences out of evil motives, but their ignorance makes them vulnerable to being duped by the realities they understand so poorly. Economists and political scientists—and for that matter, anthropologists of a certain theoretical bent (see Harris 1966)—are not slow to reinterpret religion in purely economic terms, just as political scientists are tempted to look for power games in the religions, and sociologists tend to see nothing in religion but a socially useful social institution. I am not arguing that these elements are totally absent from the religious field, but the reductionism I have described in Chapter 3 makes these "this-worldly" things all there is to religion.

And in odd and disquieting ways, some of the most enthusiastic proponents of religion—specifically, of Christianity—have partly swallowed this nonsense, to the detriment of the church. The sorriest example known to me is in the movement to "market" the church. Here, the church is represented as producing something—the gospel—that it is trying to market to consumers. For this to work, it has to be accepted that (a) the gospel is a consumer product; (b) this means that those features of the gospel that appeal to the tastes and preferences of consumers must

be highlighted, and those features that might disturb consumers must be relegated to the fine print or omitted; (c)
the church is a service agency intended to serve the desires
of consumers; (d) the church's success can be measured
precisely by how well it sells its product, that is, by how
many people it brings in; and (e) the preferences of consumers are the final determinant of what the church is
about. Ironically, this trend is built on an originally sound
perception, due partly to missionary anthropology and
emphasized by Church Growth Theory, that the felt needs
of people are the best starting point for the presentation of
the gospel. But church marketers have taken a fatal further
step: the felt needs of people are not only the starting point;
they are also the terminus. Kenneson and Street (1997)
have described with devastating insight how destructive
this stance is with respect to authenticity in the church
and with respect to true discipleship and accountability.

In the political domain, the ignorance of American
church leaders, including many theologians and missiologists, as well as denominational administrators and minis-
ters of congregations, has left the American church sadly
bereft of guidance. As a result, the great majority of
American Christians are little different from non-Christians
in the political stances they take and the rationales and
rationalizations they offer to justify their opinions. There is
a kind of de facto alliance between Christian "conservatism" and secular "conservatism," as there is between
Christian "liberalism" and secular "liberalism" (note that I
put "conservative" and "liberal" in quotation marks, for I do
not believe they have any substantive content or coherence). Christians who are drawn for any number of reasons
to the right end of the theological spectrum gravitate
uncritically to the right end of the political spectrum and
adopt its positions; the same goes on at the left end of the
respective spectra. But what is today called conservatism is
not a coherent array of integrated stances that focus on a

determinate central value; rather, it is little more than a defensive nostalgia for a past that never really existed, in which everyone was supposedly a good Christian and a good citizen (the two being virtually synonymous), and in which the true intentions of the Founding Fathers were expressed in a close alliance between church and state. Never mind that most of the Founding Fathers were deists or free thinkers; that in the decades of the founding of the nation, Christianity was at an all-time low in America; and that it was they who devised the separation between church and state. At the so-called liberal end, a similar thing occurs; liberalism in its current form is essentially a readiness to jettison the past and to tinker ad lib with society. The incoherence of both configurations can be seen most strikingly in their attitudes toward death and killing: "conservatives" tend to be bitterly opposed to the killing of infants in the womb, but they tend to be vociferously in favor of the death penalty and are often militantly in favor of warlike measures; "liberals," on the other hand, tend to be "pro choice" in relation to abortion but against war and against the death penalty. Few people notice the inconsistencies; among those who have, however, are the American Catholic bishops, who have propounded a strong and consistent pro-life policy.

The fundamental discrepancies between *both* right and left positions, as defined in the American political arena, and the kingdom of God can be seen by a more careful reading of the Sermon on the Mount. But American Christians have been well schooled in the antibiblical notion that economics and politics operate under their own rules, autonomously from the rule of God. Any serious missiology that wants to bring the gospel of the kingdom of God to bear in the lives of Americans will have to face these issues squarely.

5

The Issues

The relationship between the gospel, the church, the missionary task, and the social sciences is a highly complex one that does not lend itself to simple explanation. As has been pointed out many times, the modern scientific enterprise rests on several foundational worldview components that are themselves derived from the biblical faith: the idea that the universe is an orderly reality; that human beings have a position of authority and responsibility in the universe; and that the human mind in the exercise of its responsibility needs to, and is able to, come to an adequate understanding of the way the universe works. It has been alleged that the environmental catastrophe that impends over us is the fault of Christianity; but it is better understood to be attributable to an exaggeration of human authority and control coupled with rejection of accountability to God, which aberrations are fruits of the modern mindset. Nevertheless, Christians have much to be thankful for as we contemplate the many benefits we derive from the physical sciences and their applications in medicine, agriculture, communications, transportation, and so on. Few of us, however suspicious we might be of the modern project, would be willing to return to the lives of our ancestors five hundred or even one hundred years ago. Philip J.

Hefner (1998:52) has described eloquently how science and technology can witness "to the greatness incarnate in human life" and serve as "the soil in which the incarnate greatness grows." He singles out (biological) evolution as a powerful statement of God's work in creation; he also calls for us today to reject the two-separate-tracks view of the relation between science and gospel, as well as the view that they conflict, and to interweave our understanding of the gospel and of the universe in ways parallel to those used by the biblical writers in their time. But even Hefner points to the ambiguity of science and technology, and he does not really refer to the social sciences at all.

Nevertheless, we have already documented, if only too briefly, some of the ways in which the social sciences have been used by missiology in its efforts to improve both the understanding and the performance of the work of missions. But all of this represents the barest beginning of the fruit that could be borne by a more active and profound interaction between missiology and all of the social sciences, especially as missiology begins to take seriously the philosophical issues raised by the social sciences and the theological implications of these issues. This is especially true of a missiology addressed to the Western world, because the social sciences represent an important mode of the intellectual and moral climate of the modern and postmodern West. It is surely idle to suppose that one has a grasp on the mind—or minds—of the West if one is not wrestling in depth with the conceptual foundations of the social sciences. Both in their specific effects in the academic world and in their diffused impact on the general *Zeitgeist*, the social sciences—all of them—constitute one of the arenas of choice in the struggle for the Western soul. So the social sciences are far more than a neutral "objective" can opener to gain access to a putative "Western culture" that exists apart from the tools of inquiry. These disciplines represent in a particularly concentrated form some of the essential contents of Western culture, especially as regards some of the central properties of both secularization and secularism.

Christian Critiques of the Social Sciences

Before looking at the critiques themselves, it may be useful to mention briefly an effort early in this century to bring theology and the social sciences, especially sociology, together into a positive synthesis. The German theologian Ernst Troeltsch attempted a massive combination of liberal theology à la Harnack and evolutionary sociology under the title *Die Soziallehren der christlichen Kirchen und Gruppen* (1911; English, *The Social Teaching of the Christian Churches*). In Troeltsch's scheme, Western civilization was both Christian and superior to all others, whereas lesser societies followed lesser religions. It was not clear whether the West was culturally superior because it was Christian, or Christian because it was culturally superior. But not long after Troeltsch, the liberal theology he championed was discredited by World War I, to be replaced by the radical theology of Barth; and evolutionary sociology was displaced by functionalism, making issues of superiority or inferiority moot.

Now for a quick look at some of the critiques of the social sciences that have already appeared in the last couple of decades. Characteristically, these have been done, not by missiologists, but by Christian people themselves involved in these sciences. Some of them are extremely valuable.

Ironically, I know of no such critique of cultural anthropology. A number of Christian anthropologists, most of them deeply involved in mission, have written excellent standard textbooks in anthropology (Hiebert 1976), and even more of them have written from different perspectives about how anthropology has been and continues to be useful for cross-cultural mission. But none actually examines the philosophical foundations of the discipline with any degree of profundity or rigor. It would seem that anthropology is a philosophically neutral discipline with no problems worth mentioning!

I have already mentioned the critiques of economics by Schumacher (1973) and by Goudzwaard and de Lange (1986), which focus on the social and ethical issues occasioned by a hard-nosed application of neoclassical economics, and especially the needless pain and suffering caused for the poor and powerless peoples of the world by, for example, the recommendations of the International Monetary Fund to the bankrupt governments of Third-World countries. The call is for an economics of compassion, an "economics as if people mattered," to use Schumacher's telling phrase. But the only critic I know of who addresses the discipline as a whole and calls into question the philosophical foundations on which it is built, the taken-for-granted worldview assumptions that underlie it, is Jane Collier (1992).

I know of no comparable Christian critique of political science, though there are numerous valuable works dealing with political issues from a Christian perspective.

A small book by the French Protestant sociologist Frédéric de Coninck (1992) does an excellent job of critiquing sociology. After an opening chapter in which he demonstrates how sociology can throw light on certain biblical passages, he raises the question of how Christians can be both "not of the world" and yet very much "in the world." He proposes that the Christian's involvement take the form of three movements, encapsulated in three verbs: "come out," "dwell in," and "renew." "Come out" does not mean to absent ourselves from the world, but to detach oneself, to abandon the illusions of the world's perspectives, to become critically analytical (using sociology!). One thus asks, What is "the world?" (his analysis of *kosmos* parallels mine in an earlier chapter); one becomes critical of the world's definition and use of power, both in politics and economics (he raises the troubling question for the church: "Are we bothered because evil is oppressing people, or are we bothered because *we* do not have power?" [32]). "Dwelling" involves such things as recognizing the ambiguities of the world, dealing mercifully with them, and loving our enemies. Finally, "renewing" calls for moving from analysis to action in the world, guided by our discernment of the *telos* that lies before us and carried out by a church that is itself renewed by God's Spirit.

In psychology, the best work I have found is Mary Stewart Van Leeuwen's *The Person in Psychology* (1985). Herself a social psychologist, she spends the first part of her book spelling out how any view of "the person" rests upon some metaphysics, whether explicit or implicit. To this end, she explores ancient Greek philosophy, Asian worldviews, and modern and postmodern metaphysics, showing their consequences for personhood. Early, she points out that "within the various theoretical systems of psychology there is a marked tendency to view the person in either reduced or inflated terms" (xi). At one point she makes a trenchant observation, in the context of a discussion of the Fall: "Seen in this light, it is true on one level to say that all psychology is 'abnormal' psychology, if what we mean is that none of us functions as God originally intended us to" (51). Methodologically, she scores the double standard used almost automatically by scientists, especially behaviorists: "The problem with such a position [i.e., behaviorism] is not just its attribution of too *little* responsibility to ordinary people but its implicit attribution of too *much* responsibility to the social scientist" (121).

I have not done justice to these two profoundly insightful works, but I trust I have given enough of their flavor to move the reader to consult them personally.

But by all odds the most comprehensive, the most thorough, and the most profound of the Christian critiques of

the social sciences taken as a whole is the work by John
Milbank, *Theology and Social Theory* (1990). Moving from
Machiavelli and Hobbes on through to present-day decon-
structionists like Foucault and Lyotard, and including both
the philosophes of the eighteenth century and the scientists
of the nineteenth and early twentieth centuries, he shows
how a neglect of transcendence led all of these thinkers to
combinations of circular thinking, special pleading, non
sequiturs, and the like. But he also points out that a
Christian critique cannot rest on a modern, positivist epistemology, to which too many conservative Christians are
tempted to appeal: the postmodern critique of this epistemology is too devastatingly successful to permit any such
nostalgic strategy. But the postmodern critique itself offers
no real solutions to the human predicament, despite claims
to the contrary by some, such as Rorty. Postmodernism has
done a thorough and necessary job of demolition, but we
must look elsewhere for constructive answers. We must
look forward and find our certainty, not in a watertight
interpretation of either texts or world, but in the truthfulness and faithfulness of God, who will never disappoint us.

We may recall from Chapter 1 that the central question
at issue has to do with the nature of "the world" and the
nature of "humankind." With this in mind, I will discuss
briefly the debates between missiology and the social sciences in terms of six issues, going back in part to the
Enlightenment: (1) human origins and human nature; (2)
freedom versus determinism; (3) objectivity, (4) cultural
relativity; (5) single-cause explanations and premature
generalizations; and (6) methodological agnosticism.
Because of the limits of space and of my own knowledge, I
will deal almost entirely with the English-speaking world,
and especially the United States. Others can say better
than I whether my model applies also to the European context. It will become evident as the discussion progresses
that these six issues are all interrelated in complex ways.

Human Origins and Human Nature

It is crucial at the beginning of our discussion to distinguish between at least three kinds of concepts, all purporting to explain aspects of human reality, all called "evolution." There is first of all biological evolution, which places the human species, *Homo sapiens sapiens*, integrally into the animal kingdom, and specifically as a member of the order of primates, along with lemurs, monkeys, and apes. This is the kind of evolution that is rightly associated with the name of Darwin and has popularly been caricatured as "the descent of humans from apes." But the picture is much more complicated than that. What is suggested—with a great deal of fossil evidence, evidence from comparative anatomy, evidence from comparison of DNA, and evidence from studies of animal and human behavior and communication, among others—is that the human species did over a period of millions of years evolve gradually from earlier species, such as the *Australopithicenes* (almost all in eastern and southern Africa), *Homo erectus*, and earlier forms of *Homo sapiens*, now all extinct. The mechanisms presupposed, though far more sophisticated than those proposed by Darwin in 1859, are in principle essentially the same. This model strongly stresses the close kinship between humans and other animals, and downplays any putative gap between them; this is one of the often unadmitted reasons for the popularity of evolutionism in its ideological form.

Because this theory appeared to contradict categorically the account given of special divine creation in the Bible (Gen 1–2), understood literally, it became at once the object of bitter attack by conservative Christians; in many quarters it remains so. The attack has been all the more fierce to the extent that the "kinship-with-animals" argument has been used by its proponents to call into question many aspects of Christian morality on the grounds that humans, like other animals, should be free to act upon their impulses. Some devout Christians have attempted to erect an alternative scientific explanation of human origins and nature, based upon a literal interpretation of Genesis 1–2, under the label "creation science." The heat of the debate has elicited extreme and careless arguments on both sides, and in the process both science and biblical interpretation have been badly abused. For instance, when polemical evolutionists vociferate that "evolution is a fact," they are misrepresenting what the term *fact* means in science. And when opponents of evolution scream that evolution is "just a theory," they fail to acknowledge that *theory*, in science, is a very serious matter indeed, as witness the theory of relativity; it is by no means an arbitrary whim or hunch. Similarly, when evolutionists argue, as some do, that evolution disproves the existence of God or of creation, they are not doing science at all, but bad theology. And "creation scientists" are not doing serious science, but dubious exegesis, when they make Genesis answer questions that never entered the mind of the human authors. It seems to me that serious biblical interpretation must take into account what the different kinds of biblical texts are intended to do, and must not make them answer questions that did not even exist when they were written. I suggest that if one examines the highly complex, repetitive structure of Genesis 1, one will see that this structure points to a liturgical/mnemonic purpose for this text, not a historical-reportorial purpose. Close scrutiny shows that the text is arranged in a two-by-three pattern:

Day 1: light	**Day 4:** luminaries
Day 2: separation of sky, earth, and water	**Day 5:** flying and swimming creatures
Day 3: plants	**Day 6:** land creatures, humans

Furthermore, the error directly addressed in this chapter of Genesis was not modern evolutionism but ancient nature worship, in which the great entities of creation were gods and goddesses. Genesis 1 makes a powerful case that these things are not divine but the creation of a God who is altogether Other, and they are designed to serve the divine purpose. The whole is couched in terms of the cosmology of that day, not any of the later cosmologies that Christians have had to deal with historically: the Ptolemaic, the Copernican, the Newtonian, or the Einsteinian. Ironically, when the church did commit itself to a specific cosmology, in the Galileo controversy, it supported that of Ptolemy rather than any of those actually found in the biblical text; and in that instance the church made a fool of itself. Might this be a useful cautionary tale? Today, theologians at the right end of the spectrum have again committed themselves, unfortunately, to the extremely impoverished modern epistemology that reduces Truth to the single dimension of Fact. Their only disagreement with the secular view is as to what counts as "fact." But the biblical texts present truth in a number of guises, not all of them factual, and one needs to recognize this to do responsible biblical interpretation.

Science, for its part, must stick to its rigorous limits as to what it can claim to have explained or to have proved. Under these circumstances, I see no real contradiction between the concept that biological evolution might have been the process by which God brought us into the world, and that it was God who did the whole thing and planted in us the divine image, which sharply distinguishes between us and the other creatures. But neither do I think we should lose any sleep if some of the nontheologically motivated attacks upon evolutionism should turn out to be true, for example that of Behe (1996). Behe's argument is based strictly on his assessment of the extreme statistical improbability of some of the complex co-occurring mutations that the evolutionary schema requires to make it work.

The second type of evolution that occupied the stage of scientific thought from the mid-nineteenth century to the early twentieth, is the sort of rigid, one-size-fits-all model of social and cultural evolution associated with the names of Tylor, Morgan, and Spencer, which assumed that modern Western culture was at the summit of the single universal evolutionary ladder and that other peoples were at lower points on the same ladder. Because this form of evolution was used to support racism and colonialism, and because it has proved to be completely at odds with the empirical evidence, it has rightly been rejected by everyone. It seems to me that when Christians focused their attack on biological evolution and swallowed whole the "social Darwinism" that underlies much racism, ethnocentrism, and rejection of "the other," they were guilty of pursuing a red herring. Nevertheless, a kind of survival of social Darwinism can be found in ideologically pure laissez-faire economics, which calls for unchecked competition and, consequently, the economic survival of the fittest only.

But the third type of evolution takes into account the reality of change, especially technological change, over time; it also takes into account the generally cumulative nature of that change; and it takes with great seriousness the fact that, especially in the modern world, any given innovation might arise almost anywhere in the world and be borrowed elsewhere in the world in very short order. Thus, in the medieval period, technical and scientific ideas were borrowed wholesale by western Europe from the Far East (gunpowder, etc.) and the Middle East (e.g., the concept of zero); in the early modern period, astronomers from Bohemia, Denmark, and Italy stimulated each other; and mathematicians from England, France, and the Netherlands bounced ideas off each other. Today, improvements in medicine, manufacturing, and agriculture can originate anywhere, including the non-Western parts of the world.

The fruits of technological evolution can be, and have been, badly abused. We have only to look at the growing ecological catastrophe that is upon us. Technique, as Ellul reminded us (1970), can be an expression of human arrogance, a kind of twentieth-century Tower of Babel, in defiance of God, and a tool of the dominance of some humans over other humans. But it does not need to be thus misused. That is an illegitimate purpose brought about by the sinfulness of humans and their institutions. Technology can and will be redeemed, along with all the other fruits of human endeavor, in the City of God.

Freedom Versus Determinism

One of the features of the pre-Enlightenment Western worldview was that the universe, including the world of human institutions, was created by divine fiat and existed in conformity with the divine will. Even when the creative agency of God was minimized or rejected, the world was the way it was, not subject to human intervention or alteration.

But when God was finally banished completely from the scene in the early nineteenth century (cf. the French physicist Laplace's word to Napoleon: "Sire, I have no need of the God hypothesis"), this left the universe a totally closed system, operating by means of an unbroken chain of mechanical causes-and-effects—in other words, a fully deterministic world. In such a world, as envisioned by Isaac Newton, for instance, everything operated by means of automatic, exceptionless processes called "laws of nature," such as the laws of gravitation or thermodynamics. In such a world, one can say, "Given physical conditions A, X will occur"; and it does, every time. Quarks and molecules and nebulae do not behave one way today and another way tomorrow.

Subtly, the Enlightenment modified the ancient and medieval concept of "Natural Law" (see Simon 1965) in the direction of the newer concept of "Laws of Nature." "Natural Law," in other words, was supposed to be applicable to the world of human experience and human institutions in much the same way as "Laws of Nature" applied to the inanimate entities of the universe. But human beings, though under certain limited conditions it is possible to predict statistically what many of them will do in the mass, are quite liable to act unpredictably in any given instance; and this, not because of mere randomness as with the motion of atoms, but because of the reality of freedom and purpose. In other words, because human beings seem to exercise at least some measure of free will and even of perverseness, there can be and are empirical deviations from Natural Law. This fact has made it necessary and possible to appeal to Natural Law to redress instances of such deviation. This kind of appeal was, though of course expressed in much more high-flown rhetoric, the rationale for both the American and French Revolutions.

In other words, when modern science banished teleology, the consideration of purpose, from the universe it studied, and reduced its concern to pure cause-and-effect factors, it systematically precluded the possibility of achieving true understanding of human behavior, to the extent that the exclusion was followed rigorously. In the social sciences, the elimination of freedom and purpose from the field of study would be tantamount to reducing human beings to the same level as inanimate things. And of course many disastrous consequences would flow from this reduction, if it were carried out with ruthless rigor. As a matter of fact, social scientists generally did banish teleology at the macrolevel (e.g., God's involvement in history), but retained in varying degrees a place at the microlevel for the freedom and intentionality of individuals and groups.

People are indeed heavily conditioned by their genetic endowment, by the specific family conditions under which they grow up, by the broader cultural setting in which they live, and by the specific experiences that they undergo. Heredity provides a panoply of potentials and a fairly flexible set of outer limits. Nurture and other environmental factors favor the actual realization of some of the potentials and tend to discourage others. But within whatever possibilities and limits circumstances set for the human person, that person has some measure of freedom to respond, to choose, to decide, and to act; and does so out of conscious purpose. And it is often this limited but very real measure of freedom and purpose that the social sciences are tempted to deny. So the determinants of human existence include heredity, nurture, *and personal choice*. And, as I have already mentioned, social scientists tend to recognize this reality to various degrees.

But the tension between the determinism implicit in the Law of Nature model and the freedom and responsibility explicit in the Lockean understanding of Natural Law has been a more or less permanent feature of the social sciences. The classic "liberal" stance, represented in quite different ways by Jefferson and Rousseau, emphasized personal human freedom and responsibility, the subordination of institutions to human will and action, and the right and duty of human beings to design and operate institutions in accordance with Natural Law. In this view, institutions were almost infinitely malleable, given proper understanding and intentions. The classic "conservative" position was in essence a recasting of the relatively deterministic medieval model of the social world, which subordinated the (sinful) individual to restraining stable institutions. The classic liberal view has dominated the American popular worldview well into this century: human beings are free and responsible, and they can be praised for acting well and blamed for acting badly.

Sometime in the nineteenth century, however, an astonishing switch began to take place. Increasingly, those who took a high view of persons and a dim view of institutions, and who were thus liberals in the classic sense, began to see institutions as oppressively determining the lives and even the consciousness of persons. One strand in Rousseau's thought, expressed notably in his *Emile*, had pointed in this direction, and Karl Marx of course played a crucial role in this transformation. So-called liberals thus began to think in terms of the need to transform institutions in order to achieve the freedom human beings deserved but lacked. An example of this critical stance with respect to institutions in economics was the development by Thorstein Veblen at the turn of the century of what he called "institutional economics." The extreme form of this line of thought can be seen in the assignment of both bad and good behavior to environmental conditions. Criminology and penology, for example, were for a long time heavily influenced by this outlook. Perhaps in reaction, so-called conservatives began to champion the freedom and responsibility of the individual, so as to be able to assign praise and blame, reward and punishment, appropriately. Criminology and penology, accordingly, have responded by becoming vindictive to the point of barbarism.

The social sciences as they emerged did not all follow the same path with respect to the issue of freedom or determinism. Anthropology and sociology both divided, and no single school in either discipline is consistent on the issue, though the proponents of any serious sense of human freedom appear to be in the minority.

Political science, on the other hand, tends to represent the view that institutions respond to human intentionality, and in fact focuses many of its studies on the way human beings exercise their freedom. Thus, studies of voting behavior are among the standard approaches in political science.

Of all the sciences, economics is the one that talks the most deterministic language; this is seen in that it is the only one that makes wide use of the term *law*. One hears, for instance, of the "law of supply and demand," which says that as prices increase, producers are willing to supply larger quantities of a product; as prices decrease, the quantity will also decrease. Human decisions do occur in situations of monopoly, where the supplier controls the market and decreases supply *in order to* raise prices. A good example is the control exercised by the De Beers company over the world market in diamonds. A less successful instance is the effort of OPEC to control supplies and prices of oil. Yet it is economics that offers us *Homo economicus*, the splendidly isolated and rational individual who analyzes the facts of the market and chooses and acts accordingly. The laws, in other words, are in fact statistical generalizations rather than laws of nature.

As for psychology, its most explicitly deterministic version is the notion of operant conditioning, stemming from behaviorism and advocated by B. F. Skinner (1971). His very title, *Beyond Freedom and Dignity*, tells it all. Yet, to illustrate the lack of consensus among practitioners, it was a psychiatrist, Karl Menninger, who raised the haunting question in the title of a book: *Whatever Became of Sin?* (1973).

An interesting realization dawns upon one as one examines the literature: all of the social scientists, including the most deterministic like Skinner, make a tacit exception for their own work. They, unlike the rest of humankind, are free, and their concepts and models are not determined by their genes or their life conditions. If this were not the case, all of the findings of these scholars would have no more significance than a sneeze, for they would be nothing more than the products of determinate and determining causes (see, e.g., Van Leeuwen 1985).

One additional remark: where the social sciences tend to speak of our being determined by heredity, by nurture, or whatever, the New Testament speaks rather of our being enslaved—enslaved to our own passions and appetites (e.g., Rom 6:12–14; 7:4–12; Gal 5:19–21), and enslaved to current worldly patterns of thought and behavior (Rom. 12:2). In other words, the "freedom" that the social sciences on occasion promise but cannot deliver, freedom to do whatever one's impulses dictate, the New Testament calls servitude to sin. And it instead promises true freedom—the freedom to be what we were designed to be, servants of God. This occurs when we are identified with Christ's death and resurrection in baptism (Rom 6:1–11), and it is made possible by the Holy Spirit (Gal 5:22–24).

I do not need to belabor the implications of this debate and all the confusions and obfuscations that characterize it for the theological question of human freedom, and thus of sin, guilt, ability to understand and respond to the gospel, and the like. This question is central to any understanding of Western culture as a whole. There are also implications for the proper understanding of the possibilities of the social sciences: if determinism reigns, then the social sciences could potentially permit prediction and even control over social processes, on the example of the physical sciences. This was the explicit intention of Skinner. However, if there is any significant measure of human freedom, prediction becomes more difficult and control even more so. But the notion that a science ought to be able to confer control seems to lie behind some missiological misapplications of the social sciences, which sometimes gives the impression that given enough knowledge, mission could be a kind of engineering project.

Postmodernism has at least made it clear that control is problematic: that is, even if one can achieve it, the consequences can be disastrous. Whereas the modern perspective tended to emphasize determinism to varying degrees, the postmodern one tends to emphasize chance and randomness. The major metanarratives that defined the modern project were shown to be tools of oppressive domination of the many by the few. Order is inherently tyrannical: long live anarchy and chaos! And because everything turns out to be a power game in one form or another, it is best to take all masks off and to allow the various players to fight it out, and may the strongest win. In a very odd way, we are back to Darwinism—or rather, to Nietzsche! The picture is surely overblown; but it seems to me that it bears enough truth to serve as a red flag whenever we are tempted, as Christian workers, to imagine that we fully understand what is going on, that we are in control of things, that if we push the right buttons the right results will come out at the bottom. This trap has caught a number of Christian thinkers, across the entire theological spectrum. It began to have its noxious effects in the missiology of Warneck (1901), Gutmann, Keysser, and others, who built their missiology on a German Romantic notion of "*Volkstum*," or "peoplehood." Its impact can be seen on the one hand in the excesses of Church Growth Theory, which rests on thoroughly modern assumptions; and it is just as true for some forms of "signs and wonders" missiology, which, to put it bluntly, treat the spirit world as so many more buttons for us to push. At the other end of the spectrum, John Hick's notion (1977) that all religions spring from the same essence, whether they acknowledge it or not, is just as much shaped by Enlightenment determinism. In between, the ruthless and sometimes cynical pragmatism of church authorities of all stripes betrays the modern mindset that dominates their thinking.

What can we Christians say to all this? We can say, for example, that human dignity can in principle arise from either of two sources: human self-assertiveness or recognition of the image of God in us. The first was, of course, the option of our first parents, which led to the mess we are in at present. It places a premium on *our* importance, *our* possessions, *our* achievements. It leads automatically to the deification of self over against God and over against other humans who are doing the same thing. It also puts at risk the real worth and dignity of all nonpossessors and all nonachievers: fetuses, infants, and children; the handicapped; the elderly and moribund; losers in competitions; and members of "lesser" races, classes, castes, or nationalities. Emphasizing the image of God, on the other hand, safeguards everyone's dignity, for it is a gift in all of us, to which none of us has contributed an iota. Especially in the West, the worth of persons derives most often from what Weber called "productive work"; those unable or unwilling to do productive work are easily and not-so-subtly devalued. In a refinement of this posture, it was argued that work produced wealth, so that wealth came to be an indicator of superiority; eventually, wealth all by itself without work (as in inherited fortunes) came to be seen as an indicator of superiority.

Objectivity

Objectivity is that value in the modern pattern of thought that is based upon a radical differentiation and distancing between the Subject (observer/investigator/ manipulator) and the Object (thing observed/investigated/manipulated). The purpose of objectivity is clear and important—to prevent the biases, prejudices, fears, and hopes of the Subject from distorting its perception of the Object. This is important, because these irrelevant personal factors do in fact often prevent people from seeing reality accurately. This is evidenced, for instance, by the immense weight of racist misrepresentations that often distort our views of certain Others.

The considerable positive values of objectivity have to do, then, with discerning what is the case and dealing with it fairly, disregarding irrelevant considerations. Justice, for instance, is presented as blindfolded, representing her refusal to be influenced by who stands before her. In medicine, objectivity is helpful both for arriving at a correct diagnosis and for preserving the sanity of doctors and nurses, who might otherwise be overwhelmed by the suffering they witness continually.

D'Andrade, an anthropologist, makes a strong case for the value of objectivity as an indispensable means of getting at the empirical truth of a situation before passing moral judgment: "I argue that anthropology's claim to moral authority rests on knowing *empirical* truths about the world and that moral models should be kept separate from objective models because moral models are counter-productive in discovering how the world works" (1995:402). He goes on to use what I might call Darwinian arguments (i.e., arguments from success) to defend objective science. D'Andrade goes on to say that those who attack objectivity in social science are doing so on the basis of a shift in meaning of the word from its true meaning as "an account which describes the object, not the describer" to "an account given without bias or self-interest" (1995:404).

The irony is that although objectivity is fairly easy to achieve when one is studying the stars or the bottom of the ocean—after all, these are quite inanimate and remote—it becomes extremely difficult when one is studying sentient creatures, especially human beings. Here one's feelings, one's values, one's attitudes inevitably intrude. The child who hears a rodent rustle outside the tent and yells, "There's a lion out there!" fails to discern what is the case because of fear. The young woman who sees only good in her boyfriend, a doting parent who can see no fault in a thoroughly bad son or daughter, fails to discern what is the case because of love; the middle-aged man who sees a glamorous youth in the mirror fails to discern what is the case because of vanity. Sometimes it is our positive feelings that deceive us, but it is usually negative feelings that distort our perceptions of the Other, as mentioned above. Advertisers and political spin doctors intentionally work to distort the customers' or voters' perceptions of reality so as to shape their responses in a desired direction. The trouble with distorted perceptions is that they lead to distorted responses, so it is extremely desirable that our views of reality be as authentic as possible.

Heilbroner (1953) points out that a number of the economists he describes, including Marx, struggled to be coldly objective in their analyses of the state of affairs. Marx's response to the state of affairs he perceived was quite another matter: it was moral outrage. But objectivity prevented him, in his view, from responding prematurely and inappropriately. Most other social scientists, at least until the vogue of postmodernism, would agree with Heilbroner and D'Andrade. In fact, anthropologists have often masked their personal feelings, friendly or hostile, toward the people they studied in their "official" reports of fieldwork in order to safeguard their status as "objective" scientists. Those who expressed their feelings freely were usually criticized by colleagues. But those feelings were nevertheless present and surely affected what they saw, whether they acknowledged it or not.

The problem with objectivity is this: when one has discerned an intolerable state of affairs and continues to be objective, when one deals with persons in an impersonal manner, one is actually depersonalizing them, which is about as bad as allowing our negative attitudes to control our relationships. This was what happened with the rich man in Luke 16; it happens frequently all over the world with bureaucrats. When this happens, we are no longer treating people as You, but as It (Buber 1970). And when persons are It rather than You, which is to say when they are mere objects, then moral obligation is lessened or eliminated, and it becomes quite possible to do anything to them: torture them, perform experiments on them, kill them, as did Hitler's people dealing with Jews; kill them, as do soldiers of most countries dealing with "enemies" in wartime; or, in a more mundane way, merely manipulate them and control them to our own advantage, as in slavery or business competition. Thus, one can treat them as badly as if one actually hated them or despised them; for dealing with humans impersonally is in fact a form of subtle contempt. Tillich wrote, "It is the temptation of science to transform everything encountered, including humans, into an object that is nothing other than an object" (1988:81).

Interestingly, Buber (1970:96–98) allows for a measure of legitimate I-It relations between humans in the realms of the economy and the state. In a sense, he says, these actually require a measure of objectivity in relationships. But this is permissible only to the extent that it is circumscribed and ultimately subsumed under the more comprehensive and essential I-You relationship.

Cultural Relativity

With respect to cultural relativity, in both its ethical and epistemological forms, anthropology has led the way, especially in recent decades. This is not surprising, because its central concern was exotic cultures in which worldviews differed radically. Functionalism, as I have shown elsewhere (Taber 1991), was strongly relativistic in both its Malinowskian (in Great Britain and the United States) and its Boasian-Kroeberian (in the United States) forms. Cultural relativity in its initial appearance in anthropology was, in a sense, innocent and benign. In fact, it was designed to combat and if possible eliminate the errors of racism and ethnocentrism and safeguard the worth and dignity of all. Anthropologists in this mode presented a sort of edenic picture of a world in which equal cultures coexisted peacefully to their mutual enrichment (a picture, by the way, not far from that of Revelation 5 in the Bible!). But this view did not take seriously the fact of unequal access to power that intrudes into relations between different groups and societies.

The sociology of knowledge, explicitly arguing on the basis of the "hermeneutics of suspicion," which goes back to Marx, Darwin, and Freud, partially corrected this oversight. At one level, the main difference between them is that anthropology argues that it is culture that grounds the differences, whereas sociology argues that it is position in a social system. But the difference is less than meets the eye: social position is the outward, empirically available manifestation of the reality under question; culture is the inner, mental representation of that reality. But a deeper difference is that the sociology of knowledge assigns high significance to differences in access to power as important generators of differences in worldview, because each group wants to look as good as possible. It turns out to be especially dominant groups, wanting to justify their dominance, who produce distorted worldviews.

The process has been completed by postmodernists, as I have just pointed out in my discussion of freedom versus determinism. Postmodernists reject all forms of universal discourse, which they call "metanarratives," as inherently expressions of dominance by some over others. Whoever has the clout to define reality wins and thereby gains control. No definition is "the right one." All are relative to the interests and ambitions of its holders, so all must be debunked—or "deconstructed." Of none is this more true than is that of the modern project, with its universalizing aspirations, which in earlier centuries fostered the colonial system, today fosters the crushingly oppressive global market, and throughout history has justified the domination of the weak by the strong, of women by men, and so on. There is no truth; as Nietzsche said, there is only the "will to power," and therefore the confrontation of powers. As I have said elsewhere:

> The postmodernists are right, after all, to identify and denounce those many situations in which reality, especially social reality, as well as right and wrong, have been defined and legitimated by an exercise of power rather than persuasion. But they, together with their master Nietzsche, shared a passionate hostility toward Christianity, and so found themselves unable to construct any positive approach to either modern epistemology or modern ethics. They came to emphasize that knowledge, belief, and values on the part of persons and groups were inevitably determined by the person's or group's position in the hierarchies of the world, so that in the end defining "reality" became an exercise

in sheer power. Milbank argues persuasively that postmodernists, whatever their differences, share in common these dominant concepts: "a historicist 'genealogy,' . . . an 'ontology of difference,' . . . and 'ethical nihilism'" (Milbank 1990:278). What he means is that the postmodernists deny that anything might be permanent or universal in human experience, that the differences between persons and groups override commonalities, and that there is no foundation for any substantive ethics beyond the will-to-power. "No universals are ascribed to human society save one: that it is always a field of warfare" (Milbank 1990:282). But postmodernism, it seems to me, by discrediting modernity, does demonstrate the bankruptcy, indeed the folly, of modernity's attempt, alluded to above, to reap the fruits of the gospel while denying its roots (Taber 2001).

The debate regarding relativism has indeed been surrounded by questions about putative universals and their potential, if any, to give rise to dependable absolutes. The issues are deeply confused and confusing; but they are both highly diagnostic of the Western mind set in postmodernism and unavoidably crucial for any understanding of the way the gospel relates to very human modes of expression and communication. Hatch (1983), as I pointed out earlier, "distinguishes . . . between types of relativism; his terms are 'ethical relativism,' the 'relativism of knowledge,' 'historical relativism,' and 'methodological relativism'" (Taber 1991:114–15). He raises the question of limits to relativism but offers no answer to the dilemma.

One noxious consequence of the whole relativity debate, especially affecting anthropology, has been that if there is no such thing as fact, if there is no such thing as truth, then the distinction between reporting and fiction vanishes, and it is perfectly legitimate for an anthropologist to write a quasi-novel and present it as a report on fieldwork.

The situation has in fact arisen, to the embarrassment of more than one American university. It is also the case that the exotic culture being studied becomes, not an object in its own right with traits to be noted and respected, but a sort of Rorschach inkblot about which the anthropologist can give what amounts to no more than his or her personal impressions and feelings; anthropologists can—and do—say whatever comes into their heads, and who is to say that they are not right?

Closely related to these considerations is the "critique of ideology," which is part of the agenda of people whose agendas are shaped by the masters of suspicion. I think this issue is of great importance, especially for North American Christians, who may well be the most ideologically naive of all Christians, when they seek to gain a measure of critical distance from the forms and structures of the fallen world. For in my view, the critique of ideology comes closer than any other single secular human effort to approximating the demands of Romans 12:2—to free us from the dominant ideology of the age.

So how does one *as a Christian* resolve the issues involved here? I do not think there is a hard-and-fast response to that question. To that extent, I think that the postmodernists are right. I can make only a few suggestions, from the standpoint of what has been called "Christian critical realism."

First, variation in epistemological stance is limited by the existence of a "real world" out there. Any epistemology that hinders its proponents from coping effectively with that real world is deficient. But how deficient can it be and still function acceptably? Might one argue, for instance, that even devout Buddhists are obliged to shelve their views regarding the illusory nature of matter when they are concerned with making a living in the material world? Various peoples, including the peoples of the Bible, have operated on the basis of a wide variety of beliefs regarding the nature and causes of disease and the most appropriate therapies, and have survived as peoples, though sometimes with minimal success; and it has often been thought that it is the duty of those who have more effective knowledge in this regard to make their superior knowledge available to more benighted peoples. This was a major motivation for medical and educational missions. On the other hand, modern Western medicine has proved to be less than omniscient and omnicompetent, and the wisest scientists in the field have begun to learn in some respects from practitioners operating within alternative models.

With respect to ethical relativity, it seems clear to me that neither radical relativism nor rigid uniformity is an option. As I mentioned in an earlier chapter, even the most radical relativists reject Hitler's "final solution" but have a hard time laying a foundation for their rejection. It is difficult to make a case for "universal human rights," for instance, if one is a relativist.

It is a lot easier to talk about human rights, and even to promote them vigorously and sincerely, than to ground them adequately so as to make them validly universal. *Philosophically*, the concept of human rights—by which I mean rights that inhere in every human being and cannot be increased or diminished by such factors as "race," nationality, class or caste, sex, age, degree of wholeness, or productivity—can be secure only if grounded in immutable transcendence—which, biblically, means the doctrine of the image of God. Otherwise, it is contingent upon specific human cultures. Nor is it safe when its Christian foundations erode. *Historically*, a strong case could be made out that this concept arose only in areas heavily influenced by the Judeo-Christian story. In fact, one could argue that it— or rather the more fundamental concept of human dignity— was invented by Jesus of Nazareth on the basis of prior values proclaimed by the prophets of ancient Israel. Both in Jesus' teaching and in his concrete relationships with people, he made it clear that all human beings possessed the dignity that came to them from the hand of the Creator. Nowhere else in the world, as far as I can tell, has that radical idea arisen to any prominence.

The concept has survived in the West only as the long shadow of Christian faith, though it has not always been fully understood or practiced. Those Deists who wrote in the American Declaration of Independence about "unalienable rights" rightly attribute them to "their Creator"; but the rights mentioned were in fact limited to white adult propertied males, and it has taken over two centuries of yet-to-be-completed struggle to extend these rights to all American citizens. The atheists who brought about the French Revolution and wrote a grandiloquent document about the "universal rights of man" were not slow to violate these rights on a huge scale at the guillotine.

Today, relativists who want to insist on universal human rights are arguing, therefore, on the basis of the residue of Christian influence that originally shaped the ethical outlook of the West; in other words, they are either crypto-Christians or Western cultural imperialists—as people from non-Western cultures are not slow to point out from time to time. It turns out to be difficult, if not impossible, to find a solid ground for a serious respect for human dignity apart from the biblical teaching regarding the image of God. We see this vividly today in the eroding respect for "nonproductive" humans, such as unborn infants, severely damaged persons, and terminally ill persons. Abortion, euthanasia, and the abuse of the handicapped are all gaining increasing acceptance in a society that is less and less shaped by biblical values, and that appeals only to "humanistic" ethics for its understanding of "human rights."

The same is true for those who want to insist that any or all of the religions—taking only "the best" of each—can fill the bill as ground for a unanimous understanding of human rights. But who decides what is "the best"? And on what basis? And it is patently not true that all religions share the same respect for the dignity of all humans. One has only to look to one of the ethical giants of this century, Mohandas Gandhi, to see this: determined as he was to respect all humans, he could not truly transcend the caste system that is integral to Hinduism.

On the other hand, ethical absolutists also have a hard time justifying their position, because even if one wants to found ethics on the Bible one must admit a degree of relativism in the interpretive process. After all, the positions stated in the Bible, Old and New Testaments, are rooted in specific historical situations and are therefore culturally conditioned; moreover, the contemporary interpreter is also culturally conditioned in the hermeneutical process.

But every culture has ethical rules; and, if one delves beneath the surface, many of the most basic rules look astonishingly like the second table of the Decalogue: "Honor your father and your mother. . . . You shall not kill. You shall not commit adultery. You shall not steal. You shall not bear false witness. . . . You shall not covet [that which is your neighbor's]" (Exod 12–17). It seems to me that all of the undoubted differences between the ethical codes of different cultures are matters of interpretation and application of these most fundamental principles. A major question is this: Under what circumstances, and in relation to what people, do the rules apply? Many cultures prescribe quite rigorous rules for internal relations within the society, but allow for sometimes extreme exceptions in dealing with foreigners. In Don Richardson's *Peace Child* (1974), we are introduced to the Sawi of Irian Jaya, who, according to Richardson, idealize treachery. But clearly there must be some community, even if it is of minimal size, inside of which rules of fidelity and trust apply; otherwise, there would have been no Sawi survivors for Richardson to address. It turns out that the difference between the Sawi and Americans is that we have to travel farther to find someone whom it's acceptable to kill; and when we do, as a society, kill (as in war), we do it wholesale rather than retail. It is not clear to me that the Sawi are any more "savage" than we are. But the point is that every society, for its mere survival, must have rules of the sort summarized in the last six of the Ten Commandments.

But this means that relations with the Other are problematic; which, of course, surprises none of us, given what we see daily on television. Virtually any dimension of difference—"race," nationality, ethnicity, culture, class, caste, age, sex—can pit us against one another. It seems as though we no sooner seem to overcome one noxious ground of discrimination—say, "race"—than another takes its place in the popular imagination. Incidentally, as long as anthropologists—and missiologists who follow them—deal with peoples and communities as isolates, they will be ill equipped to propose solutions to the problems arising from relations between groups.

Single-Cause Explanations and Premature Generalizations

Another tendency in the social sciences, fortunately now passing from the scene, also attributable to the pressures for "scientific" economy and elegance, is the tendency to advance single-cause explanations for complex realities in the human world. This is closely related to the disciplinary reductionism discussed toward the end of Chapter 3. The roots of this powerful tendency in the sciences go back a long way, to the medieval philosopher Ockham. Ockham argued that one should not, in attempting to explain anything, invoke more dimensions or components than absolutely necessary. This criterion came to be called "Ockham's razor." To put it in extreme terms, an explanation should not be more complicated than the thing it is explaining. In other words, economy, often called parsimony in the literature, is a strong value in science. One of the major reasons why Einstein's Theory of Relativity was so immediately appealing to his fellow-scientists is the extreme economy and elegance of that majestic formula: $E = MC^2$.

So social scientists have attempted to follow suit. Economists, for instance, describe human beings as if they were exclusively producers and consumers of goods and services. This makes for simplicity in the claims and assertions of economists; but it also makes their "explanations" of economic behavior less than credible, because all of us know very well that in the real world we act—we buy and sell, for instance—out of a complex and shifting mixture of motives and reasons, not merely out of a calculated and purely economic motive. Our noneconomic beliefs, attitudes, and values impinge unsystematically but powerfully on our economic behavior. Similarly, psychology and its therapeutic offshoots are arbitrarily tying their own hands behind their backs when they consider the individual without taking stock of the web of social connections in which the individual is located. Social psychology is emphasizing this, but it is my impression that clinical psychologists and psychiatrists often do not take this factor with enough seriousness.

The most blatant example of single-cause explanations that have been advanced in the human sciences is expressed in the debate between heredity and nurture as *the* cause of all human traits and behaviors. Fortunately, this debate is about over within the sciences, but its long shadow remains influential in popular thinking, as evidenced by the comic movie *Trading Places*.

But it is becoming increasingly clear that, when one is dealing with the human sphere, very little occurs that has a single "cause." Even in our bodies, physicians are recognizing that many diseases come about through a concatenation of circumstances working together: for instance, genetic predisposition, lifestyle, and external provocative agents (e.g., bacteria, secondary tobacco smoke). It seems to me highly improbable that any single factor can be said to "cause" such complex human patterns as intelligence, athletic ability, sexual orientation, criminality, and the like; yet some scholars keep trying to find such simple causes, as in the perennial debate about the supposed causative role of "race" in relation to intelligence, and the perennial search for "the criminal gene."

In their push to formulate "scientific" statements, some social scientists sometimes make premature sweeping generalizations that ignore cultural differences between peoples or other variables that happen to be outside the orbit of their interests. This is most true of economics, political science, and to a large extent psychology, which commonly act and speak as if human beings and their institutions were exactly the same around the world regardless of the specific cultural conditioning that shaped them. Sociology is a bit more sophisticated in this regard, for sociologists do try to consider systems and structures with some degree of wholeness, and they are bound to recognize the existence of cultural ideas that alter things that would otherwise be the same. And many sociologists have actually studied non-Western societies with ample recognition of the difference that culture makes. Anthropologists should, of course, be immune to the error of ignoring cultural differences, for culture, and more specifically cultural diversity, is their field of study. For the most part, they are; in fact, many of them join sociologists of knowledge and postmodern decontructionists in so emphasizing the relativity of points of view that they lapse into radical relativism. Yet even in anthropology, there have been pressures to make the discipline a "nomothetic" science, that is, one that formulates supposedly universal "laws" of human behavior. One especially amusing instance is the work of Marvin Harris, a historical materialist, who accomplished the astonishing *tour de force*—as well as *reductio ad absurdum*—of "explaining" the phenomenon of

sacred cows in India as a purely logical economic phenomenon in which religion played no real role (1966).

Methodological Agnosticism

But the overarching error of social scientists, following the
example of natural scientists, is, of course, their methodological agnosticism, which is intimately connected with
the view of the universe as a closed system, operating under
the immanent laws of cause-and-effect that we mentioned
earlier. Purpose or finality are by definition excluded, as is
creation by a personal God. But when God is banished from
the world in the name of science, what emerges, ironically,
is a new pantheism in the guise of science—the worship of
"Nature" as self-existent, obeying its own immanent laws.
In fact, the modern scientific pantheism displays some of
the features of the Hindu doctrine of *karma*, notably its
inevitable character—but without any trace of the moral
dimension of *karma*. The Jesuit theologian Avery Dulles
makes this point, citing John Paul II:

> The world must be reminded, he says, that while
> men and women can organize the world without
> God, *without* God it will always, in the last analysis,
> be organized *against humanity*. In denying the tran-
> scendent source and goal of our being, we would
> deprive man of the source of his true dignity. . . .
> Without God as creator there would be no inviolable
> human rights (Dulles 1993:6).

As it happens, a great majority of social scientists in the
West are personally either agnostics or atheists. But for the
most part, even those who are Christian or Jewish or
Muslim believers, when they act and speak in their roles as
"scientists," find themselves bound by and committed to
the limiting condition "as if God did not exist." This is
because of the powerful pressure of empiricism and logical
positivism in the social sciences, even as it has been all but

abandoned in the philosophy of science and even to some extent in the physical sciences. This fact no doubt reflects the persistent insecurity of social scientists in the face of the condescension of "real," that is, physical, scientists.

But this is ironic, for in all creation human beings are the one sort of thing that cannot in any sense be seriously accounted for apart from the reality of God: we were, after all, created in the very image and likeness of God. If our Godlikeness is left out of account, then we are in fact no more than especially clever apes; ethics and morality then have lost any solid foundation, and true sociality becomes impossible. For if one thing is clear, even in purely this-worldly terms, it is that we human beings are not genetically determined to act in the best interests of our group, let alone of humankind in general. If any restraints and constraints on our antisocial impulses in fact exist, they are founded on a laboriously constructed cultural edifice. And if this edifice is fragile, as it is when it loses the ultimate divine sanction and people no longer submit to it willingly, then the demon in us is turned loose and society self-destructs, and our superior cleverness becomes not an advantage but a fatal disadvantage.

The final paradox is that, if God is not in the picture, these clever animals that we are must fill the vacuum left by the banishment of God. We are not only animals, we are gods! Or rather, perhaps, we in the mass are animals, but the scientists who have banished God and freed us from our ancient delusions have become gods. Could anything be more terrifying?

I therefore conclude: any account of the human condition, individually, collectively, and globally, that does not take into account the createdness, the Godlikeness, and the sinfulness of humankind and human institutions will fail in the task of explanation. And any design for human living that is not controlled by the vision of the coming kingdom of God is bound to fail to produce a liveable world.

But the Gospel . . .

It would be bad enough if the bankruptcy involved in the collapse of the modern project were merely philosophical, as it may seem to have been in my discussion. Postmodernism has indeed shown that the modern emperor has no clothes, but has proved unable to cover the emperor's nakedness. The fallout is catastrophic in terms of human life at all levels: personal, interpersonal, communal, societal, international, global. Modernity banished purpose, and therefore meaning, except at the microlevel; postmodernism has not recovered it. Modernity banished freedom while claiming to foster it, and therefore has banished responsibility; and postmodernism has offered no help. Without freedom and responsibility, there can be no forgiveness of sin (cf. Menninger 1973); modernity and postmodernity can offer to deny the reality of sin only spuriously. Modernity has created the monadic individual, destroying community; and postmodernism has merely aggravated the problem. So human beings are doomed to an existence without meaning or purpose, without dignity, freedom, or responsibility, without forgiveness, without community. No wonder they give up in apathy or despair, or strike out in pointless rage, or try desperately to gain some recognition (Warhol's "15 minutes of fame") by doing the gratuitously absurd or outrageous, or simply lapse into "Eat, drink, and be merry; for tomorrow we die." Similarly, the "autonomous" human social sphere postulated by secular thinkers from Hobbes on is, exactly like the "autonomous" individual, anomalous and pathological, because it is willfully alienated from the source of its true being and reality. Is there no exit from this closed world bent on self-destruction? Is there no hope?

Here, it seems to me, is precisely where the gospel is at its most powerful and its most persuasive: when it breaks open the closed world and finds God at work in it; when it insists that human beings, however related biologically to other creatures, are unique in having in them "the image of God," which confers dignity without the need for any contribution on their part, so that it belongs equally to the unborn, to the totally disabled, to the senile, as well as to the able, "productive" person; when it describes a God who loves God's creatures unconditionally and is ready to forgive them by sheer grace and mercy; when it promises, and delivers, real freedom in place of our captivity to the powers or to our appetites; when it makes of us children of God, and then co-laborers with God in God's magnificent project to reclaim the desolate creation and restore it to God's own benevolent rule for which it was designed in the first place; when it insists, in other words, that we have before us, not mindless optimism, but HOPE.

To put it another way: in a world where all existing candidates for the status of global "metanarrative," especially the modern one, have been effectively debunked by postmodernism as mere power games by which some people try to dominate other people, the gospel is the one metanarrative that is not and cannot be threatening, because it is offered to us by a king whose throne is a cross. The Good News is that God's king is the only one who desires exclusively our good: our freedom, our joy, our security. He is the only one who offers himself sacrificially as the agent of our restoration to God's original design for us, that we should enjoy fellowship with God and participation in God's bliss forever.

But for this message to be credible, the church will have to think and act differently than is often the case today. It will need to be more humble, less self-confident. The church, after all, is, like the redeemed persons who compose it, *on the way* to restoration to the purposes and blessings of God. It has not arrived, any more than its individual members, and, like them, it displays in varying degrees the marks of its "not yet perfected" character.

The church also betrays its true nature when it accepts the role of being one corporate body, one institution in society among others, playing by the rules that control the secular world and using the world's means of power to achieve allegedly spiritual ends. It is precisely to the extent that it does this that it *can* be empirically and accurately described by sociology, which is the science of *fallen*, that is, *pathological*, social realities.

But this gospel will be credible in this world only if it is *incarnated* as it was in Jesus himself, in the people to whom Jesus said, "As the Father has sent me, so I send you" (John 20:21). Just talking about it will accomplish nothing; people are disillusioned by mere talk. It will not be accomplished by taking thought and devising effective and efficient methods, which was the approach of modernity. It will not be accomplished by debunking our "competitors," whether "liberals," "conservatives," "communists," "reactionaries"—or the other religions of the world. It will not be accomplished, especially in this postmodern world, by a church still captive to modern patterns of thought and action, to modern ways of analyzing reality, to modern ways of planning work, to the modern addiction to management and control. The church needs to be less concerned with correctly dotting all the doctrinal "i's" and correctly crossing all the methodological "t's," and more concerned to live Christ in the power of the Holy Spirit. Our offer of the gospel can be credible only if it comes to people from a community that is intentionally and intensively patterned, in thought, word, and deed, on its Lord. This community will be one without worldly power (for worldly power inevitably corrupts us and distorts our message) and without worldly ambitions (for even church growth can be a quite worldly ambition!). It will be a community, in other words, that has died to self, that has died to the world, and that lives the new life of Jesus in the Spirit.

Missiological Postlude

So how are we to conclude? How might the social sciences, flawed as we have seen them to be, be used to design and implement an appropriate missiology for the Western world? It might seem, as I have described and criticized them, that these sciences are so flawed, so confused and mistaken in what they allege about the world, that they can be of no use to us. But this would be a serious misunderstanding. I would maintain that the social sciences are indeed often in error or superficial, but by no means always! They can, in fact, help us in many ways, as when they jolt us out of erroneous but prevalent popular views of the way things are, the way things work. They offer us innumerable valid insights that will enrich and deepen our missiology. And their very mistakes can be enlightening to the serious and critical student, because they are symptoms of what ails the West.

Missiology, like all endeavors that we undertake in behalf of the kingdom of God, is often forced to move beyond its secure knowledge in order to accomplish anything. It often skates on very thin ice. It cannot afford, therefore, to overlook any potentially useful instruments to improve its understanding and performance. The social sciences, used responsibly and critically, are clearly such instruments.

References Cited

NOTE: Classic works through the nineteenth century that are mentioned in the text by way of illustration will not be further listed here.

Behe, Michael J. 1996. *Darwin's Black Box: The Biochemical Challenge to Evolution*. New York: The Free Press.

Beidelman, T. O. 1982. *Colonial Evangelism*. Bloomington: Indiana University Press.

Benedict, Ruth. 1946. *The Chrysanthemum and the Sword*. Boston: Houghton Mifflin.

Berger, Peter L., and Thomas Luckmann. 1967. *The Social Construction of Reality*. Garden City: Anchor Books.

Boas, Franz. 1940. *Race, Language and Culture*. New York: The Free Press.

Bonk, Jonathan J. 1991. *Missions and Money: Affluence as a Western Missionary Problem*. Maryknoll: Orbis Books.

Bosch, David J. 1991. *Transforming Mission*. Maryknoll: Orbis Books.

Boulding, Kenneth E. 1969. Economics as a Moral Science. *American Economic Review* 61/1:1–12.

——. 1973. *The Economy of Love and Fear*. Belmont, Calif.: Wadsworth.

Buber, Martin. 1970. *I and Thou*. Trans. by Walter Kaufmann. New York: Charles Scribner's Sons.

Bull, Hedley. 1966. International Theory: The Case for a Classical Approach. *World Politics* (April 1966):361–77.

Clooney, Francis X. 1990. Roberto de Nobili: Adaptation and Reasonable Interpretation of Religion. *Missiology* 18:25–36.

Codrington, R. H. 1891. *The Melanesians*. Oxford: The Clarendon Press.

Collier, Jane. 1992. Contemporary Culture and the Role of Economics. In *The Gospel and Contemporary Culture*. Ed. Hugh Montefiore, 103–28. London: Mowbray.

Coninck, Frédéric de. 1992. *Ethique chrétienne et sociologie*. Méry-sur-Oise, France: Editions Sator.

D'Andrade, Roy. 1995. Moral Models in Anthropology. *Current Anthropology* 36/1:399–420.

Dennis, James S. 1897, 1899, 1906. *Christian Missions and Social Progress*. 3 vols. New York: Fleming H. Revell.

DiNoia, Joseph. 1992. *The Diversity of Religions*. Washington, D.C.: Catholic University of America Press.

Donovan, Vincent J. 1982. *Christianity Rediscovered: An Epistle from the Masai*. Maryknoll: Orbis Books.

Douglas, Mary, and Steven Ney. 1998. *Missing Persons*. Berkeley: University of California Press.

Dries, Angelyn. 1998. *The Missionary Movement in American Catholic History*. Maryknoll: Orbis Books.

Dulles, Avery. 1993. The Prophetic Humanism of John Paul II. *America* (Oct. 23, 1993):6–11.

Durkheim, Emile. 1961. *The Elementary Forms of the Religious Life*. Trans. John Ward Swain. New York: Collins Books (orig. 1915).

Easton, David. 1968. Political Science. *International Encyclopedia of the Social Sciences*. Ed. David L. Sills. Vol. 12. New York: Macmillan. Pp. 282–98.

Ellul, Jacques. 1970. *The Technological Society*. Trans. John Wilkinson. New York: Alfred A. Knopf.

——. 1991. *Anarchy and Christianity*. Trans. Geoffrey W. Bromiley. Grand Rapids: Eerdmans.

Freeman, Derek. 1983. *Margaret Mead in Samoa: The Making and Unmaking of an Anthropological Myth*. Cambridge: Harvard University Press.

Goudzwaard, Bob, and Harry de Lange. 1986. *Beyond Poverty and Affluence: Toward an Economy of Care*. Grand Rapids: Eerdmans.

Habermas, Jürgen. 1971. *Knowledge and Human Interests*. Trans. Jeremy J. Shapiro. Boston: Beacon Press.

——. 1973. *Theory and Practice*. Trans. John Viertel. Boston: Beacon Press.

Harris, George. 1868. *On Foreign Missions in Connection with Civilization and Anthropology*. London: Bell and Daldy.

Harris, Marvin. 1966. The Cultural Ecology of India's Sacred Cattle. *Current Anthropology* 7/1.

——. 1968. *The Rise of Anthropological Theory*. New York: Columbia University Press.

Hatch, Elvin. 1983. *Culture and Morality: The Relativity of Values in Anthropology*. New York: Columbia University Press.

Hefner, Philip J. 1998. Science, Technology and Christian Faith: The Warp and Weft of Mission. *Mission Studies* 15/2:51–65.

Heilbroner, Robert L. 1953. *The Worldly Philosophers*. New York: Simon & Schuster.

——. 1995. Weighing the Human Interest Rate. *Harper's Monthly* (March 1995):18–22.

Heim, S. Mark. 1995. *Salvations*. Maryknoll: Orbis Books.

Hekman, Susan J. 1986. H*ermeneutics and the Sociology of Knowledge*. Notre Dame: University of Notre Dame Press.

Herskovits, Melville J. 1973. *Cultural Relativism*. Ed. Frances Herskovits. New York: Vintage Books.

Hick, John. 1977. *The Myth of God Incarnate*. London: SCM Press.

Hiebert, Paul G. 1976. *Cultural Anthropology*. Philadelphia: J. B. Lippincott.

Hocking, William E., ed. 1932. *Report of the Laymen's Enquiry on Re-Thinking Missions*. New York: Harper & Brothers.

Hopper, David H. 1991. *Technology, Theology, and the Idea of Progress*. Louisville: Westminster/John Knox Press.

International Encyclopedia of the Social Sciences. 1968. 19 vols. Ed. David L. Sills. New York: Macmillan.

James, William. 1902. *The Varieties of Religious Experience*. New York: Random House.

Junod, Henri. 1927. *The Life of a South African Tribe*. 2 vols. London: Macmillan.

Kaplan, Morton A. 1969. The New Great Debate: Traditionalism vs. Science in International Relations. *Contending Approaches to International Relations*. Ed. Klaus Knox and James M. Rosenau. Princeton: Princeton University Press.

Keesing, Roger M. 1976. *Cultural Anthropology: A Contemporary Perspective*. New York: Holt, Rinehart & Winston.

Kenneson, Philip D., and James L. Street. 1997. *Selling Out the Church: The Dangers of Church Marketing*. Nashville: Abingdon Press.

Knitter, Paul J. 1985. *No Other Name?* Maryknoll: Orbis Books.

Kraft, Charles H. 1979. *Christianity in Culture*. Maryknoll: Orbis Books.

Krass, Alfred E. 1978. *Five Lanterns at Sundown*. Grand Rapids: Eerdmans.

Kroeber, Alfred. 1948. *Anthropology*. Rev. ed. New York: Harcourt Brace Jovanovich.

Kroeber, Alfred L., and Clyde Kluckhohn. 1952. *Culture: A Critical Review of Concepts and Definitions.* Anthropology Papers 47/1. Cambridge, Mass: Peabody Museum.

Kuhn, Thomas S. 1970. *The Structure of Scientific Revolutions.* 2nd ed. Revised. Chicago: University of Chicago Press.

Kuper, Adam. 1988. *The Invention of Primitive Society: The Making and Unmaking of an Illusion.* London and New York: Routledge.

Lasch, Christopher. 1991. *The True and Only Heaven.* New York: W. W. Norton.

Latourette, Kenneth Scott. 1970. *A History of the Expansion of Christianity.* 6 vols. Grand Rapids: Zondervan (orig. 1937–1944).

Laver, Michael. 1983. *Politics.* Oxford: Blackwell.

Leenhardt, Maurice. 1979. *Do Kamo: Person and Myth in Melanesia.* Trans. Basia Miller Gulati. Chicago: University of Chicago Press.

Luzbetak, Louis J. 1988. *The Church and Cultures: New Perspectives in Missionary Anthropology.* Maryknoll: Orbis Books.

Lyman, Stanford M. 1978. *The Seven Deadly Sins: Society and Evil.* New York: St. Martin's Press.

Malinowski, Bronislav. 1922. *Argonauts of the Western Pacific.* London: Routledge.

McGavran, Donald A. 1955. *The Bridges of God.* New York: Friendship Press.

——. 1970. *Understanding Church Growth.* Grand Rapids: Eerdmans.

Mead, Margaret. 1928. *Coming of Age in Samoa.* New York: William Morrow.

Menninger, Karl. 1973. *Whatever Became of Sin?* New York: Hawthorn Books.

Milbank, John. 1990. *Theology and Social Theory.* Oxford: Blackwell.

Minogue, Kenneth. 1995. *Politics: A Very Short Introduction*. Oxford and New York: Oxford University Press.

Munch, Richard, and Neil J. Smelser, eds. 1992. *Theory of Culture*. Berkeley: University of California Press.

Myrdal, Gunnar. 1944. *An American Dilemma*. New York: Harper & Row.

Neill, Stephen. 1964. *A History of Christian Missions*. Harmondsworth, Eng.: Penguin Books.

Nida, Eugene A., and Charles R. Taber. 1969. *Theory and Practice of Translation*. Leiden, Neth.: E. J. Brill.

Oden, Thomas C. 1983. *Pastoral Theology: The Essentials of Ministry*. San Francisco: Harper & Row.

Polanyi, Michael. 1958. *Personal Knowledge*. Chicago: University of Chicago Press.

Preus, Samuel J. 1987. *Explaining Religion*. New Haven: Yale University Press.

Priest, Robert J. 1986–87. Anthropologists and Missionaries, Moral Roots of Conflict. *Journal of Christian Reconstruction* 11/2:216–42.

Radcliffe-Brown, 1922. *The Andaman Islanders*. Cambridge: Cambridge University Press.

Richardson, Don. 1974. *Peace Child*. Glendale, Calif.: Regal Books Division, G/L Publications.

Robert, Dana L. 1996. *American Women in Mission: A Social History of Their Thought and Practice*. Macon, Ga.: Mercer University Press.

Sanderson, Stephen K., ed. 1995. *Civilization and World Systems: Studying World Historical Change*. Walnut Creek, Calif.: AltaMira Press.

Sanneh, Lamin. 1990. *Translating the Message*. Maryknoll: Orbis Books.

Schmidt, Wilhelm. 1939. *The Culture Historical Method of Ethnology*. Trans. S. A. Seeker. New York: Fortuny.

Schreiter, Robert J. 1984. *Constructing Local Theologies*. Maryknoll: Orbis Books.

Schumacher, E. F. 1973. *Small Is Beautiful: Economics as if People Mattered*. New York: Harper & Row.

Shenk, Wilbert R. 1996. The Role of Theory in Mission Studies. *Missiology* 24:31–46.

Simon, Yves R. 1965. *The Tradition of Natural Law*. New York: Fordham University Press.

Skinner, B. F., 1971. *Beyond Freedom and Dignity*. New York: Alfred A. Knopf.

Smalley, William A. 1991. *Translation as Mission*. Maryknoll: Orbis Books.

Smith, Edwin W. 1924. Social Anthropology and Mission Work. *International Review of Missions* 13:518–31.

Somit, Albert, and Joseph Tanenhaus. 1982. *The Development of American Political Science*. New York: Irvington Publications.

Spengler, Oswald. 1934. *The Decline of the West*. Trans. Charles Francis Atkinson. London: G. Allen & Unwin.

Stackhouse, Max. 1984. *Creeds, Society, and Human Rights*. Grand Rapids: Eerdmans.

Stanley, Sam. 1975. The Panajachel Symposium. *Current Anthropology* 16/4:518–24.

Steward, Julian. 1955. *A Theory of Culture Change*. Urbana: University of Illinois Press.

Stipe, Claude E. 1980. Anthropologists versus Missionaries: The Influence of Presuppositions. With comments by Ethel Boissevain, Ronald J. Burwell, Vinigi Grottanelli, Jean Guiart, Hermann Hochegger, Rodolfo Larios Nunez, Lucy Mair, Martin Mluanda, William H. Newell, Martin Ottenheimer, Glenn T. Petersen, Delbert Rice, Michael A. Rynkiewich, Frank A. Salamone, Robert B. Taylor, Julio Teran-Dutari, Paul R. Turner, Adriaan C. VanOss, and reply by the author. *Current Anthropology* 21:165–79.

Taber, Charles R. 1991. *The World Is Too Much With Us*. Macon, Ga.: Mercer University Press.

——. 2001. "Globalization and the Gospel." In *A Scandalous Prophet*. Ed. Thomas Foust, Andrew Kirk, Werner Ustorf, and George R. Hunsberger. Grand Rapids: Eerdmans.

Tawney, R. H. 1926. *Religion and the Rise of Capitalism*. New York: Harcourt, Brace & Co.

Tax, Sol. 1975. Action Anthropology. *Current Anthropology* 16/4:514–17.

Tillich, Paul. 1988. *The Spiritual Situation in Our Technical Society*. Macon, Ga.: Mercer University Press.

Van Leeuwen, Mary Stewart. 1985. *The Person in Psychology: A Contemporary Christian Appraisal*. Grand Rapids: Eerdmans.

Warneck, Gustav. 1901. *Outline of a History of Protestant Missions from the Reformation to the Present Time*. Trans. George Robson. New York: Fleming H. Revell.

Weber, Max. 1947. *The Protestant Ethic and the Spirit of Capitalism*. Trans. Talcott Parsons. New York: The Free Press.

White, Leslie A. 1959. *The Evolution of Culture*. New York: McGraw-Hill.

Whiteman, Darrell L., ed. 1985. *Missionaries, Anthropologists, and Culture Change*. Vol. 1. Williamsburg: Department of Anthropology, College of William and Mary.

Wink, Walter. 1992. *Engaging the Powers*. Minneapolis: Fortress Press.